Paul Comon

Pentax Classic Cameras

Magic Lantern Guides
Proof of Purchase
Pentax Classic
Cameras

Magic Lantern Guides

PENTAX

CLASSIC CAMERAS

Series

SPOTMATIC

Series

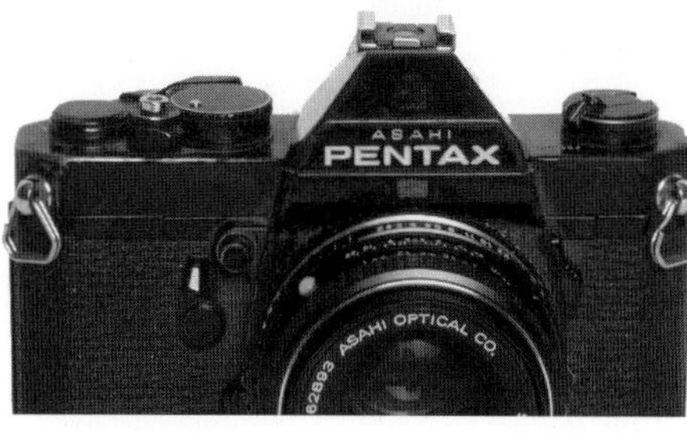

Paul Comon

Magic Lantern Guide to
Pentax Classic Cameras

A Laterna magica® book

Published in the United States of America by

Silver Pixel Press®
A Tiffen® Company
21 Jet View Drive
Rochester, NY 14624
Fax: (716) 328-5078

Written by Paul Comon
Printed in Germany by Kösel GmbH, Kempten

Library of Congress Cataloging-in-Publication Data
Comon, Paul.
Pentax classic cameras / Paul Comon.
p. cm. -- (Magic lantern guides)
"A laterna magica book."
ISBN 1-883403-53-7 (pbk.)
1. Pentax cameras -- Handbooks, manuals, etc. I. Title.
II. Series.
TR263.P4C57 1999
771.3'2 -- dc21 98-36473
CIP

Contents

Acknowledgments

Writing a book about cameras from a bygone era was more difficult than anticipated. Without the help of many good people, it would have been impossible. I wish to thank the people at the Pentax Corporation, and their parent company, Asahi Optical Company, for all their assistance.

Roger Newsham is a fund of photographic knowledge. His feedback always encourages me, and his Pentax collection was invaluable when I needed cameras to photograph as illustrations for this volume.

Most cameras appearing in this book belong to Wade Wilcox. Every accessory and lens pictured separately (plus some lenses mounted on camera bodies) also belongs to him. Wade is a walking Pentax encyclopedia. When I asked him a question, usually about obscure facts, he answered without hesitation. He rarely needs to look up any Pentax data—he remembers virtually everything. His proofreading is responsible for leading me through the technical maze.

Last but not least, I thank Shirley, my wife and best friend. No one can realize what she puts up with—me. I am truly a fortunate man.

PRC

Foreword

This book was written for everyone who owns or loves classic Asahi cameras. Historians and collectors will rediscover Asahi lore and terminology that is no longer commonly used. New Asahi fans will uncover interesting information about classic Asahi cameras, such as: What is the difference between an Asahi Pentax and a Honeywell Pentax? How many Spotmatic models are there? Everyone interested in Asahi products will want to know how its line of lenses evolved. Why were screw-mount lenses discontinued, why was the "K" series of lenses introduced, and how did they evolve into the lenses that are currently in production? All this and more can be found between the covers of this book.

Most cameras of this vintage have long outlived their instruction manuals. This comprehensive book describes the location, purpose, and uses of Asahi camera features and functions, including how to get the most out of each camera model.

And since most instruction manuals do not delve deeply into using the camera's features, you'll find many basic and advanced photographic techniques, plus tips and shortcuts for making good photographs with these wonderful classic cameras.

Most importantly, this book is about the fun of photography and the use of any fine vintage camera. Photography is the universal language, and one of the most enjoyable endeavors available to modern man. The author and publisher hope to advance this concept with this *Magic Lantern Guide to Pentax Classic Cameras*, the comprehensive guide to some of Asahi's most popular classic cameras.

Note: Dates cited in this book were established from various historical sources. Whenever possible, introduction dates were obtained from authorized United States Pentax dealer catalogs, however, data are not available on every camera model featured in this book. Some historical data were obtained from sources in both the United Kingdom and Germany; introduction dates in those countries did not (and do not) always coincide with U.S. introduction.

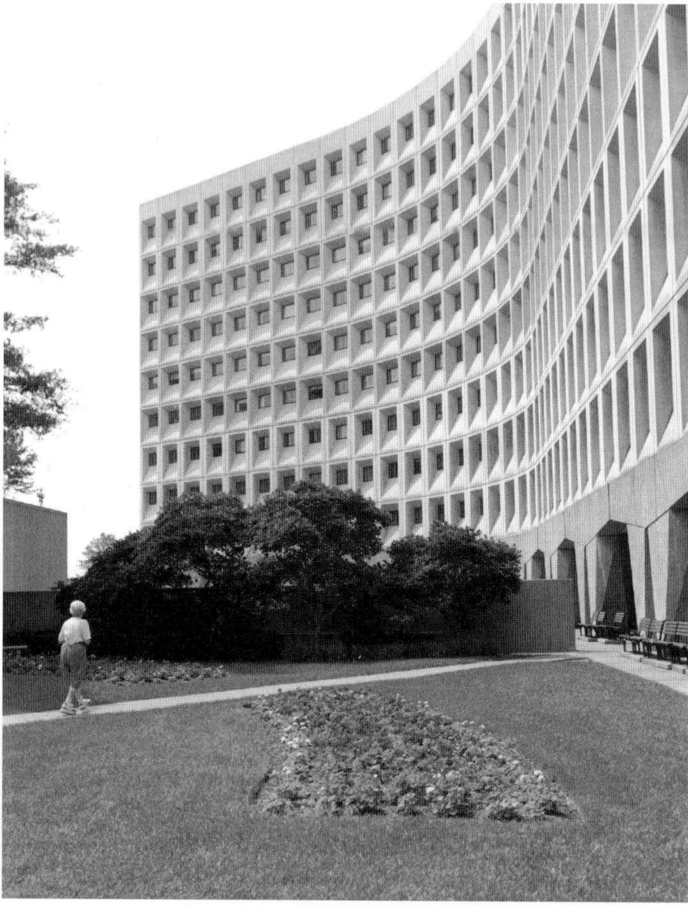

Though the architectural design of this building is strong, with its curves, lines, shadows, and angles, the addition of a human figure adds to the photo's composition. Cover the person with your hand to see what a difference it makes.

Using Your Pentax Classic Camera

Batteries for Classic Cameras

Early cameras—even the ones that contain built-in light meters—do not require batteries. First came extinction-type meters, then selenium-celled meters. Only with the advent of cadmium-celled meters were batteries required. As cameras became more sophisticated, their dependency on batteries became greater. Today, the power supply controls exposure, adjusts autofocus, fires built-in flashes, and advances and rewinds film.

Classic Pentax cameras covered in this volume use batteries in a variety of ways: to activate the light meter, control the shutter, automatically adjust exposure, or any combination of the above. The cadmium-sulfide (CdS) meters found in early Pentax cameras were typically powered by batteries that obtained their energy from an oxide of mercury. Mercury-oxide cells were, at the time, the battery of choice. They delivered an extremely uniform supply of power. Voltage in a nearly expired battery was, for all practical purposes, identical to that of a fresh cell. CdS meters were simple for manufacturers to construct and did not require the power-regulating circuitry that is necessary in the more modern meters powered by today's environmentally safe power cells.

Early in the 1990s, batteries containing mercury were banned. This caused a momentary panic—everyone interested in classic cameras was affected. But, necessity is the mother of invention. The first attempt to solve the problem resulted in alkaline-powered cells, but they were less than satisfactory. Their current flow drops within weeks, and classic meters do not contain a power regulator. Some critics say that an alkaline cell in a CdS meter is too hot the first month, just right the second, and too weak the third month.

Finally, in 1995 the so-called zinc air battery was offered for sale by Wein Products Inc. As the line of WeinCells expanded, virtually every older meter (built-in or hand-held) became useful again. These WeinCells are available at most camera stores. (For more information, or to find the WeinCell dealer nearest you, contact The Tiffen Company at 1-716-328-7800).

Many of the Pentax cameras covered in this book require S76-type batteries or the equivalent. Many manufacturers offer this type of battery; the designation usually contains the numerals 76, such as the Kodak KS76. S76 batteries are silver-oxide based. Although lithium or alkaline (A76) batteries can also be used for these cameras, we believe that silver-oxide batteries are the best investment. They supply power for a relatively long period of time, and they outperform other batteries at cold temperatures.

The chart below lists the batteries required by the Pentax camera models covered in this book. The original battery requirement, along with its replacement, is indicated. Many other equivalent batteries are available from different manufacturers. This list is by no means exhaustive.

Camera	**Battery**	**Quantity**
Spotmatic, Spotmatic II, IIa	E400N/MRB400*	1
SP 500, SP 1000	E400N/MRB400*	1
Spotmatic F	EPX625 or	
	EPX13/MRB625*	1
K2, K2 DMD	S76 or A76	2
KM	S76 or A76	1
KX, LX	S76 or A76	2
ME, ME Super	S76 or A76	2
	also 2L76	1
MEF	S76 or A76	4
MG	S76 or A76	2
	also 2L76	1
MV, MV-1	S76 or A76	1
	also 2L76	1
MX	S76 or A76	2
	also 2L76	1

**As stated earlier, most mercury batteries are no longer available. The current substitute for the E400N battery is the WeinCell MRB400; the EPX625/EPX13 is replaced by the WeinCell MRB625.*

The batteries still available for the Pentax cameras listed in this book are available from many battery manufacturers. Below is a cross-index of some of the manufacturers' battery designations.

Manufacturer	Silver	Alkaline	Lithium
Duracell	MS76	PX76A	DL1/3N
Eveready	EPX76 (S76)	A76	2L76
Kodak	KS76	KA76	K58L
Panasonic	SP76	LR44	—
Rayovac	RS76	—	—
Varta	V76PX	V13GA	CR1/3N

Battery Installation and Testing

Although all the cameras in this book have at least one mechanical shutter speed, which allows you to take pictures manually without the aid of an in-camera meter, they do require batteries to power their meters (and therefore, their Automatic exposure modes). Each camera takes different types of batteries, and each has a different method of testing battery power. See the chapter on your camera for specifics on the type of battery to use and how to test them.

The battery chamber on all of these Pentax cameras is located on the bottom of the camera. Most battery chamber covers feature a slot large enough for a coin to be inserted into it. Use a coin to unscrew and remove the cover. The Pentax MEF has a hinged battery cover door, making the use of a coin unnecessary. The battery chambers are marked with a polarity diagram to make installation easy. Match the + and – symbols on the batteries and battery chamber for proper installation.

Caution: *Never leave batteries in any camera for prolonged periods. Batteries can leak, and they are much safer stored in the refrigerator than in your camera.*

If the batteries fail and you have no replacement cells handy, these Pentax cameras can be used manually with shutter speeds of "B" or another manual shutter speed. (See the chapter on your

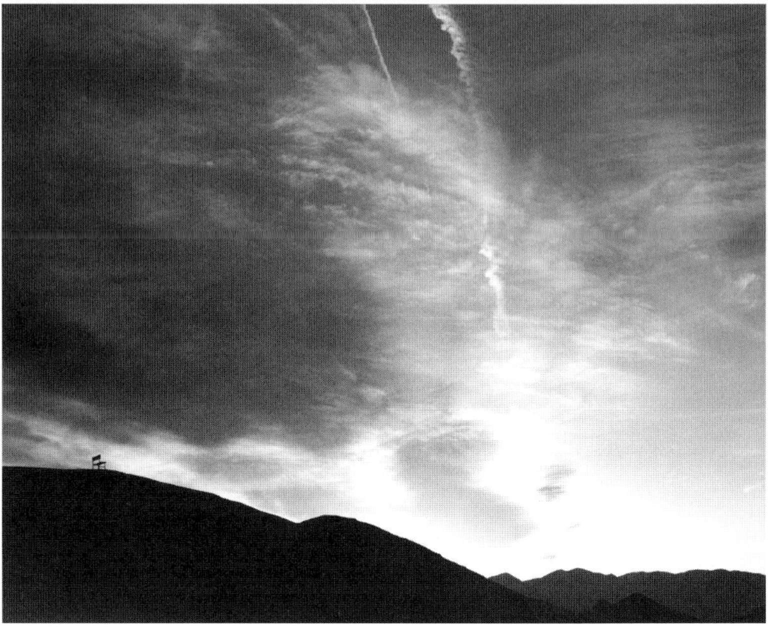

Sunsets can be as stunning in black and white as in color. The drama is in the contrast. Notice how important the silhouetted bench is to the composition.

specific camera for more information on what mechanical speeds are available). Naturally, when the batteries cannot power the light meter, you must determine exposure values some other way (e.g., hand-held meter, exposure chart, or guesstimate).

Hint: Never go on vacation without spare batteries. Cameras, electronic flash units, flashlights, and other battery-driven devices can fail at unpredictable times. Though you can often find replacement batteries in an unfamiliar location, sometimes you can't, and why waste valuable time searching?

Loading Film

The Pentax cameras in this book load and unload in basically the same way. Before opening the camera back to load a fresh roll of film, first make sure that there is no film in the camera! The easiest way to do this is to turn the rewind lever without depressing the rewind button. If the camera is loaded, the rewind crank will offer resistance caused by the tension of the film being attached to the take-up spool; a free-turning crank means the camera is empty.

To open the camera back, pull up on the rewind knob until the back springs open. Then, place the film cassette into its chamber (below the rewind knob), and press the rewind knob down so the knob's extension engages with the hole in the top of the cassette. Pull the leader out to the right, making sure that the film runs parallel to the film rails. Place the tip of the leader into a slot in the take-up spool. The film perforations should be engaged with the film advance sprockets. Wind the film advance lever until the film wraps at least once around the take-up spool to prevent the film from becoming detached. Then close the camera back.

Do not load the camera with the shutter speed dial in the "AUTO" position while the lens cap is on or while loading in a dark place as this can cause such long delays that the unsuspecting

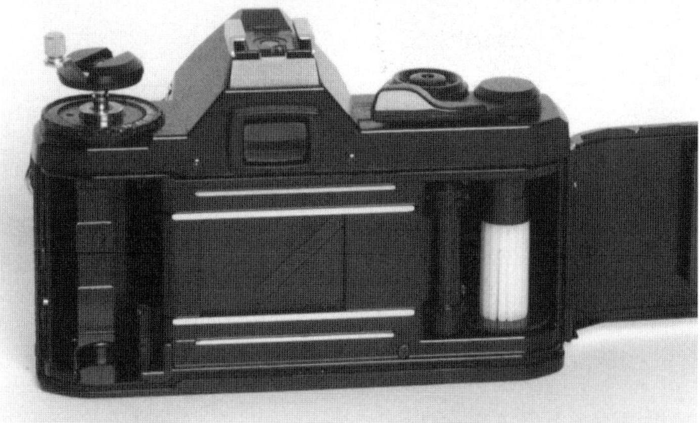

Before loading a fresh roll of film, be sure that there is no film in the camera or that the roll that is currently loaded has been rewound. Then, pull up on the rewind knob to open the camera back.

photographer may fear the camera has jammed. Select a fast manual shutter speed or the one that is marked as the X sync speed. Now advance the roll to the first frame ("1") by alternately winding the film advance lever and tripping the shutter.

The film counter automatically resets when the back of the camera is opened; it begins counting when the camera back is closed. Each time the film advance lever is wound, the counter advances one frame.

Rewinding Film

When the final exposure on the roll has been taken, or if you want to remove the roll before it is finished, follow these simple instructions. Depress the rewind button located on the camera's base, fold out the rewind crank from the film rewind knob, and rotate the crank in the direction indicated by its arrow. You do not need to continue holding in the rewind button while rewinding the film. When the film is completely rewound (you will hear and feel the film separate from the take-up spool), open the camera back and remove the film cassette.

Unloading and Reloading a Partially Exposed Roll of Film

Changing film in mid-roll is sometimes necessary, especially if the photographer has only one camera body. Sooner or later most serious shooters end up with more than one camera, but even then it may be advantageous to change films in mid-roll.

Removing a partially exposed roll is done in the same manner as removing a completed roll, with one exception: the leader should not be completely retracted. When the film comes off of the take-up spool, the separation can be heard and felt if the camera is rewound manually. All of the cameras covered in this book have manual rewind.

If the leader happens to be rewound inside the cassette, a film leader retriever (an inexpensive device found at any camera store) can be used to pull it back out. Be sure to mark the partially exposed roll with the number of frames already taken.

When you are ready to reload the partially exposed roll, first set the camera to its Manual mode with a shutter speed of 1/100 second or faster. Then, in a dark location and with a light-tight

If by accident the film leader has been completely retracted into the cassette, it can be recovered with a handy and inexpensive film leader retriever.

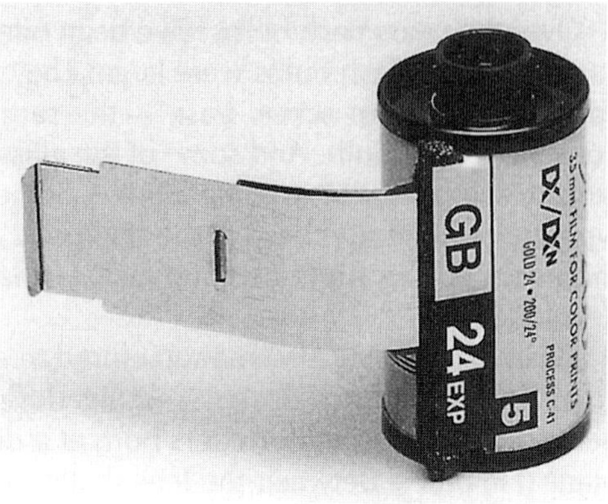

lens cap firmly in place (to avoid double exposures), load the film and advance it a frame or two past the last exposure made on the roll to prevent overlapping exposures. To advance the film, trip the shutter and wind the film repeatedly until the frame counter reads the frame number you desire. Now you can commence shooting. Mid-roll changes can be performed more than once per roll. After all the frames on the roll have been exposed, rewind the film all the way back into the cassette, open the camera back, and remove the film cassette.

Setting the Film Speed

When these Pentax cameras were being produced, film speeds were rated according to a scale called "ASA." You will see this designation marked on these cameras' film speed dials. Today's film speeds are rated according to a scale determined by the International Standards Organization, thus the film speeds are now called "ISO" values. The numerical values in both systems are identical. We have used the term ISO throughout this manual.

All film speed ratings are based upon a logarithmic progression. Every ISO dial, and all film speeds, advance in a never-

This photograph of comet Hyakutake proves that special equipment is not necessary for astrophotography. Only the basics were required: a camera, a normal lens, a tripod, and a cable release. It was taken using ISO 100 film exposed for 8 minutes at f/2.8.

changing progression, and these Pentax cameras are no exception. The higher the ISO number, the more sensitive the film is to light, or the "faster" the film is said to be. Conversely, the lower the ISO number, the less sensitive the film is, and the "slower" the film speed is said to be. The ISO film speed ratings are: 6, 8, 10, 12, 16, 20, 25, 32, 40, 50, 64, 80, 100, 125, 160, 200, 250, 320, 400, 500, 640, 800, 1000, 1250, 1600, 2000, 2500, and 3200.

Mounting and Removing a Bayonet-Mount Lens

Before mounting a bayonet-mount lens to a Pentax bayonet-mount camera, remove the camera's body cap and the rear lens cap. Align the red dots on the body and lens. Insert the lens into the body chamber and turn it clockwise (as you face the camera) until it clicks, ensuring that the lens is locked into place.

To remove the lens from the body, depress the lens release lever while turning the lens counterclockwise. Separate the lens from the body carefully to prevent damage to the mount and/or the lens. Lens and body caps should always be kept handy; keeping the lens' rear element and the camera's body cavity covered can prevent costly accidents.

Hint: Some photographers attach two rear lens caps together, back to back. This trick makes lens changing simpler, because a cap attached to another lens gives the camera user something substantial to hold onto. Lens storage also is made more convenient and efficient, because two lenses can fit into a compartment where previously only one could.

How to Hold a Camera

The person who knows how to hold a camera steadily will take sharper pictures than the one who does not. Most cameras are designed for right-handed operation; the left-handed person must resign him or herself to this fact, and once the camera has become familiar, it will make no difference.

Most controls located on the camera body are operated by the right hand, and most lens controls are set with the left hand. If the camera does not have a motor drive attached, then advancing the film and releasing the shutter are right-handed functions. Focusing and aperture control are performed with the left hand.

Note: When the terms "left" and "right" are used to describe the locations of the various camera controls, they refer to the position of the control when the camera is held in the shooting position. However, when the controls' locations are compared to a clock face (e.g., one o'clock), it is assumed that you are looking at the front of the camera.

Novice photographers generally grip the camera properly with their right hand, but are usually unaware of what their left hand should be doing. The ideal place for the left palm is under the camera. It supports the lens and acts as a base. This still leaves the left fingers free to work the necessary controls. At the moment of exposure, the left fingers should grip the lens as a further means of support. Additional support can be achieved by resting the elbows on the rib cage and the top of the camera against the forehead.

Your feet should be placed in a stance slightly wider than shoulder width—one foot slightly behind the other. A comfortable stance is a good stance. Breath control is also important to reduce the chance of camera shake. Before the exposure is made, take a deep breath, let half of it out, and then shoot.

Every person and every camera is different. Testing yourself by taking pictures at various shutter speeds will indicate the shutter speeds that can be hand-held successfully by you. There is a general rule that pictures can be shot hand-held at a shutter speed equal to or faster than the reciprocal of the focal length of the lens in use (i.e., if you are using a 250mm lens, then the slowest shutter speed that you can use hand-held would be 1/250 second). But be cautious, because there are no absolutes when it comes to determining a shutter speed that will produce sharp images. A person under pressure might perform differently than when calm. The final outcome of most tests indicates that most photographers can get clear, enlargement-quality sharpness at 1/250 second. They can almost always get a sharp image at 1/125 second, and usually get an image of acceptable sharpness at 1/60 second. At 1/30 second photographers who are especially steady can get acceptably sharp results. You can increase the odds, though, by having something steady to brace against.

When steadiness is in doubt, use additional support. Leaning against a firm, stationary object will increase stability. Leaning

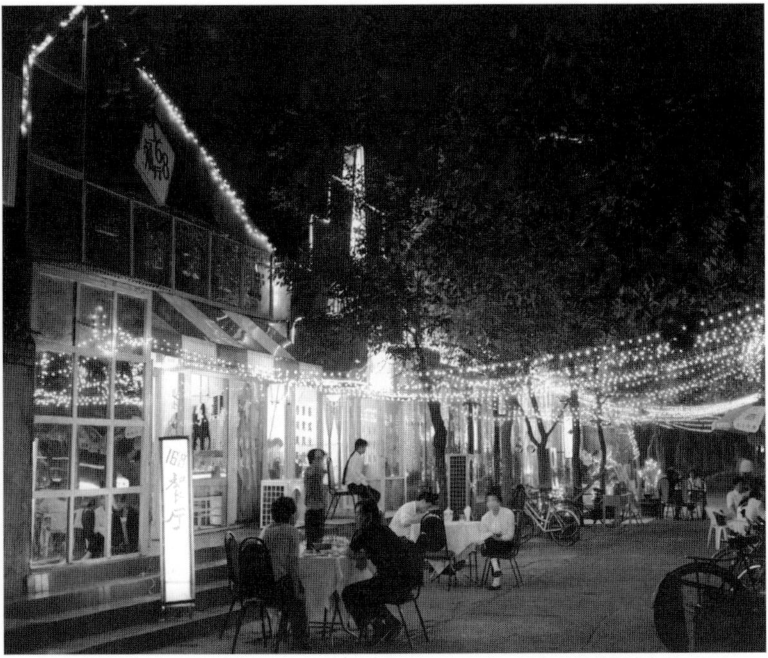

When traveling, carry a tripod, even if it must be a pocket-sized one. This time-exposure captured the flavor of the night. Exposure was 14 seconds at f/8 using ISO 100 film.

against a tree, propping elbows on a table, or using other creative supports usually pay off. The ultimate camera support is a steady tripod. Most images, when examined under high magnification, reveal that sharpness is enhanced by the use of a tripod. This is true even when fast shutter speeds are employed. When a tripod is not practical, a monopod may be an option to consider.

Shutter Speeds

We have just seen how the shutter speed and the photographer's ability to hold a camera steady relate to one another, but what shutter speed is required to stop a specific action?

If a moving object is coming straight towards the camera, a slower shutter speed can be used than if that same object traveling at the same speed travels on a path perpendicular to the camera. Distant objects can be shot at slower shutter speeds than the same action occurring closer at hand. And, all other factors being equal, telephoto lenses require faster shutter speeds than normal lenses, and normal lenses require faster shutter speeds than wide-angle lenses.

With this in mind, here are some generalities: 1/30 second and slower requires some support, 1/60 second is a marginal speed for photographing still objects, 1/125 second is the ideal shutter speed for hand-held photography of still objects, 1/250 second will probably freeze the motion of a person running, 1/500 second will freeze the motion of most horses running and may freeze a fast-moving automobile, but 1/1000 second is safer for most auto races.

Aperture Settings

Understanding lens settings is easy. Any confusion can be alleviated by considering a few simple facts.

The "f" in f/stop stands for "factor," though it's easier to think of it as standing for "fraction." Some beginners panic when they see numbers like f/1.4, f/2, f/2.8, and so on. They cannot understand why f/8 lets in more light than f/16. If the numbers were written correctly (1/8, 1/11, 1/16, and 1/22), then part of the mystery would be clear. Furthermore, any given f/stop is the fractional relationship between the diameter of the aperture and the lens' focal length. In other words, if a 50mm lens is set at f/2, the measurement of the lens aperture is 25mm (50mm x 1/2 = 25mm).

If we did the math, we would see that the aperture numbers (f/numbers) in common use are exact multiples. Following a logarithmic equation, each number in the standard series of f/numbers transmits exactly one-half the amount of light that the number that precedes it transmits: f/1.4, f/2, f/2.8, f/4, f/5.6, f/8, f/11, f/16, f/22, f/32, and so on. Other numbers like f/1.8, f/4.5, etc. are partial stops. A person really interested in the nuts and bolts of photography should memorize the numbers that represent full

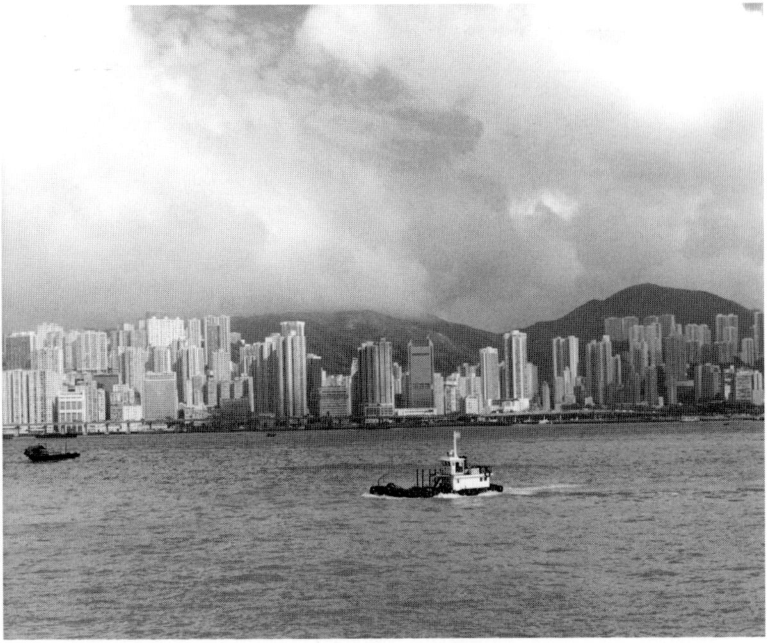

Stopping down mid-point in a lens' aperture range usually offers maximum sharpness. In this photo, the tugboat and shoreline are sharp, adding intensity to the overhead storm clouds.

f/stops. The photographer who is less interested should at least be able to look at an aperture scale and identify the full stops.

Maximum lens sharpness is usually achieved by stopping down to approximately mid-point in the lens' aperture range. Most lenses designed for use on 35mm cameras are at their sharpest when set at f/5.6, f/8, or f/11. A photograph taken with the lens set with a fully open aperture can suffer from the lens maker's inability to polish the lens' edge sufficiently. The older the lens, the more this generally holds true. Beyond the mid-point setting, another problem, defraction, can deteriorate the image. Many photographers try to stop their lens down as much as possible, believing they are achieving maximum sharpness. That is, however, incorrect. Compromise is the key.

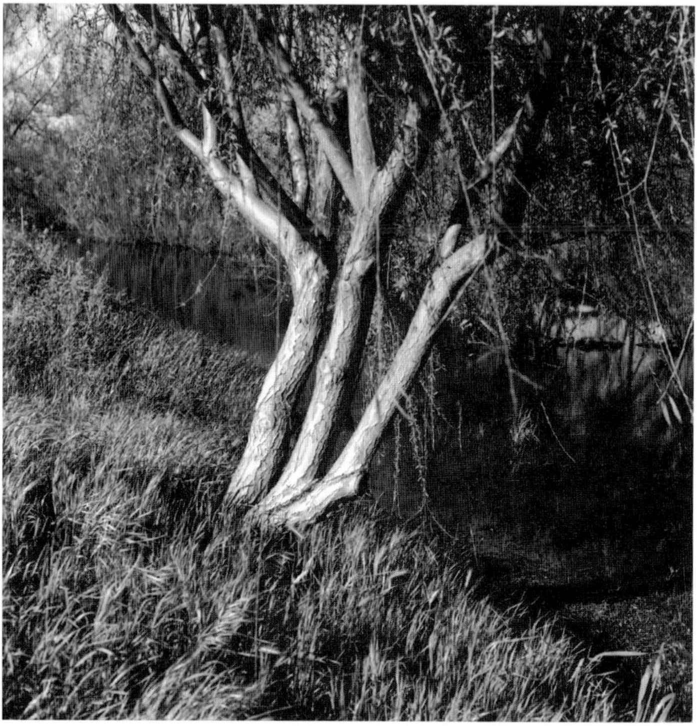

Move in close to your subject to create an interesting composition. Using the strong graphic lines of the tree trunks as the primary focal point makes for a successful photograph.

Selecting an Appropriate Film

Film comes in three types: color transparency (slide), color negative, and black-and-white negative (black-and-white transparency films exist, but they are rarely used today). Transparency film is most often used for projection, and prints from transparencies are expensive. Negative films are used primarily to produce prints. Transparencies can be made from negatives, and vice versa, but it is best to select the film that offers the desired end result. Converting from negative to slide or slide to negative is more expensive, and each additional generation reduces image quality. Slide film and negative materials are equally easy to convert to Kodak Photo CDs. Computer access to images via other means is also readily available.

Films are rated for their sensitivity to light. There have been many rating scales: Weston, Schneider, DIN, and ASA are some that have been used in the past. Finally, the entire world has adopted a film speed rating called "ISO." The numbers used for ISO and ASA film speed ratings are identical.

Greater light sensitivity is achieved by using film emulsions that contain larger silver salts. However, the larger the silver particles are, the more visible they become in the image, detracting from image quality. This effect is often called "grain." The above description is not precisely true (it is an oversimplification of this phenomenon), but it gives an adequate description, for our purposes, of what "grain" is.

All Photographic Settings Are Compromises

The factors listed below are interrelated. They should all be considered as a group when making photographic choices.

- ❑ High ISO films allow for faster shutter speeds and smaller apertures.
- ❑ High ISO films are grainier than lower ISO films.
- ❑ Fast shutter speeds more effectively freeze action and eliminate camera shake.
- ❑ Faster shutter speeds require wider apertures, if all other factors remain unchanged.
- ❑ To obtain an equivalent exposure value, when the shutter speed is increased, the aperture must be opened by an equal number of stops to compensate.
- ❑ Wider apertures allow for faster shutter speeds.
- ❑ Wide apertures usually cause reduced lens acuity* and always diminish depth of field.
- ❑ Small lens apertures also diminish lens acuity.*
- ❑ Small lens apertures increase depth of field.
- ❑ Smaller lens apertures require slower shutter speeds if all other factors remain unchanged.

Note: When manufacturing a lens, optical sharpness at the edge of the lens is harder to achieve than crown (center) sharpness. Therefore, a wide-open lens is not as sharp as one that is stopped down. Also, as a lens is stopped down, defraction (caused by the scatter of light striking the edge of the diaphragm blades) plays an increasing role in the overall sharpness (or deterioration of sharpness) of the lens. Therefore, maximum sharpness is achieved at some aperture near the middle of its scale.

Another part of the equation pertains to the focal length of the lens in use:

❑ Wide-angle lenses have more depth of field than normal (50mm) lenses, and normal lenses have more depth of field than telephoto lenses.

❑ Wide-angle lenses are easier to handhold than normal lenses or telephotos. Thought of in a different way, a telephoto magnifies everything, image size as well as body movement. And the longer the lens, the more it magnifies movement.

❑ Wide-angle lenses produce images with greater depth of field than normal and telephoto lenses do. (Technically this is not entirely correct, but for the sake of illustration, let's consider it so. Virtually every test seems to indicate that depth of field diminishes with increased focal length. Actually, the depth of field achieved by a wide-angle and a telephoto lens would be found to be similar, if not identical, if the same subject were photographed with both lenses at distances such that the subject was the same size on both frames.) Sometimes shallow depth of field is called for, and sometimes slow shutter speeds and/or image blur will produce the desired effect. Experience and compromise will yield the best possible results.

For general photography, follow these guidelines: select the slowest ISO film that will do the job, set the aperture at a midpoint setting, and then select the slowest shutter speed that will accomplish the job.

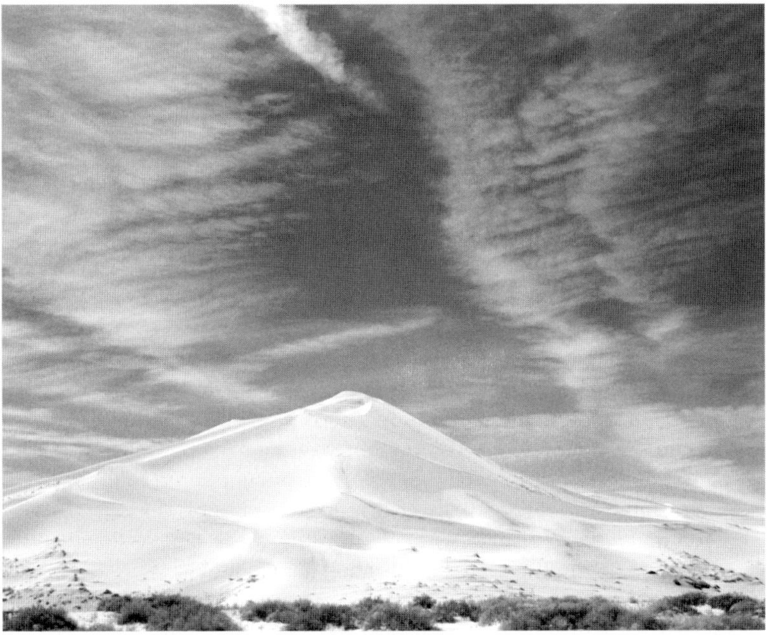

Subtle tones are achieved only when exposure is measured precisely. Metering the all-white sands would have resulted in underexposure, and there weren't enough midtones to get a good reading. In situations like this, it's wise to meter off an 18% gray card and bracket the exposure to increase your chances of getting a successful photo.

Proper Focusing Techniques

Elementary focusing techniques are simple; advanced ones require some thought. If only one plane of sharpness is required in a photograph, it would seem that a photographer need only focus there and shoot. But there is more to it than just that. Are other elements in the scene important? Are there objects in the background that are distracting? Will the entire flower, from petal tip to stem, be rendered sharply?

Before we attack these problems, let's consider the actual mechanics of focusing an SLR camera. Most cameras come with a focusing screen that is either of the split-image or microprism type. Some are equipped with both.

A split-image finder has a line dividing the center circle of the viewfinder. Out-of-focus subjects will appear to be unaligned where the circle is bisected. This is easiest to see on vertical lines or edges of objects. Focusing is accomplished by turning the lens' focusing ring until the offset parts of the image align themselves. Although the split-image rangefinder is considered best for general photography, it has serious drawbacks under certain conditions. In poor light or when used with slow lenses (f/4.5 or slower), half of the rangefinder may go dark. If this occurs, the outer area of the finder should be used for focusing.

A microprism rangefinder is usually not as easy to use as a split-image finder, but it never fails. Poor light and/or slow lenses do not affect its performance as much. When an image is badly out of focus, the image in the microprism area is doubled; when the image is focused, the double images are superimposed. A slightly out-of-focus image will "dance" or shimmer in the microprism, and a focused image will not. Some confusion can arise because a microprism is so accurate—the subject's eye may not "dance" at the same time that his cheek does.

No focusing system is ideal for every situation. Because of this, some viewfinder screens offer two focusing options, a split-image rangefinder surrounded by a microprism ring. Other cameras allow focusing screens to be interchanged. Learn to use the equipment at your disposal to its fullest advantage.

Microprism vs. Split-Image Focusing

The Pentax cameras discussed in this book were sold equipped with a microprism or a combination split-image and microprism

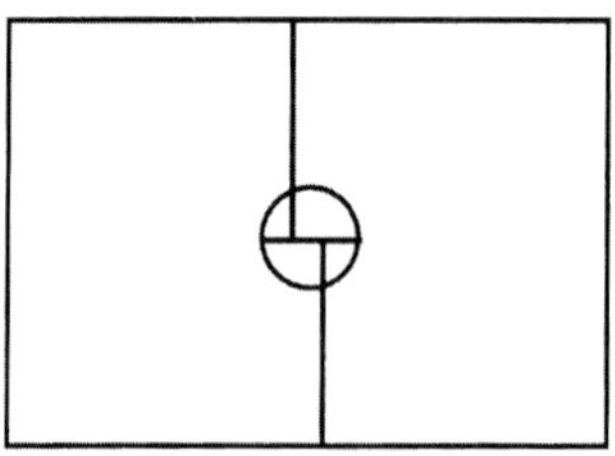

Out of Focus

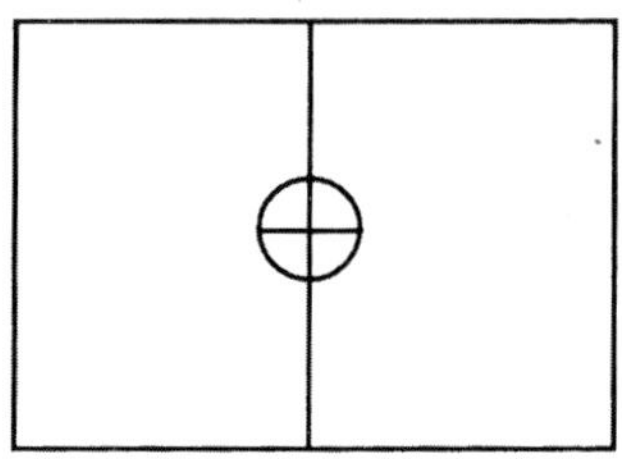

In Focus

focusing screen. Microprism focusing is accomplished by turning the lens' focusing ring until the microprism image in the center of the viewfinder is sharp. If the object in the microprism is not sharp, the microprism will break the image up into small dots, appearing to "dance." Microprism focusing is the most versatile method of focusing. Though slower than split-image focusing, it works well in low light, with long lenses, and does not require sharp-edged targets.

Split-image focusing is accomplished by turning the lens' focusing ring until the images in the top half and bottom half of the focusing circle are aligned. When the camera is held horizontally, focus to align vertical lines in the subject. When the camera is held vertically, focus to align horizontal lines.

In strong light, when using fast lenses, or when speed is required, split-image focusing is the system of choice. As conditions become less favorable, split-image focusing screens are less successful. One-half of the focusing circle will darken or "black out." When this occurs, the photographer can use the outer portion of the focusing screen, but ground-glass focusing is difficult and often unreliable.

Focusing with Infrared Film

Infrared film is different than conventional film, so taking pictures with it requires a bit of special knowledge. The rays of infrared light do not converge at the same point as those of visible light, so when taking photographs with infrared film, an additional adjustment must be made (unless the lens is infrared corrected as with the 300mm f/5.6 Ultra Achromat). First, focus in the conventional way, remember the distance indicated on the focusing ring, then readjust the focus so that the distance aligns with the red line located close to the visible light index.

Depth of Field

Up until now, we have discussed depth of field without explaining how it functions. Depth of field is part of the picture-taking compromise. It involves focus settings, aperture control, and indirectly affects the selection of shutter speed and film speed. Depth of field refers to the area that is in apparent sharp focus in any

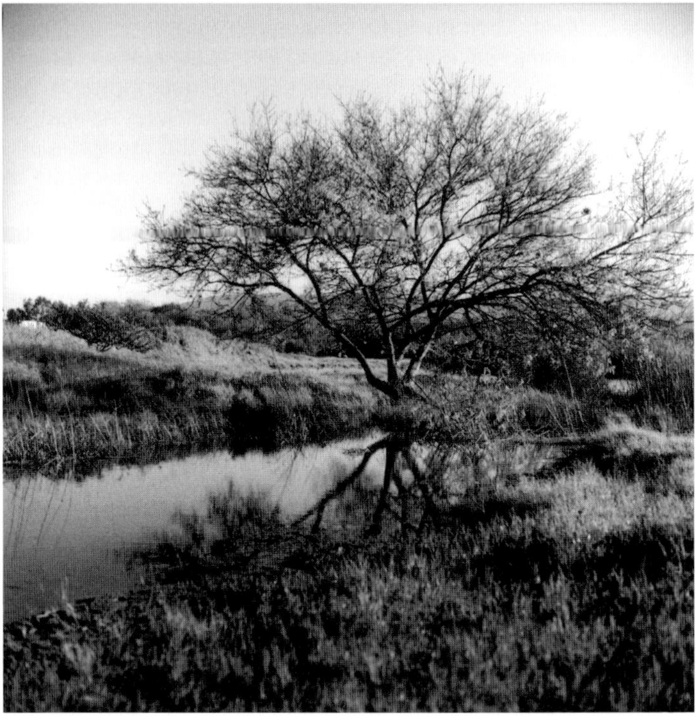

Opening up the aperture reduces depth of field. Here, a wide aperture blurs the background and isolates the tree, making it the primary focal point.

photograph. It is influenced by three factors: lens-to-subject distance, lens aperture, and lens focal length. Distant scenes photographed with short focal length lenses set at their minimum aperture will contain maximum depth of field, or in other words, the maximum range of apparent focus.

Depth of field is really not a complex concept, and understanding how it works is equally simple. When a lens is focused on any point, depth of field distributes itself in the following ratio: one-third of the total range of focus is in front of the focus point, and two-thirds of the range is behind the focus point. Because of this, a person who wants the maximum range of sharpness in a picture should not focus on infinity. This is because a lens focused on infinity is utilizing only one-third of its depth-of-field capability (the third that lies in front of infinity). Instead, the lens should be focused one-third of the way into the area of desired focus.

Most single-focal-length (non-zoom) lenses designed for use with small- and medium-format cameras contain a depth-of-field scale. Asahi-manufactured lenses usually have a scale that consists of a focus index and what appears to be duplicate aperture scales on either side of it. (There is also a smaller line on this scale, which aids in focusing on infrared film and is discussed on page 33.) The depth-of-field scale has two lines for each aperture, one on either side of the aperture index. These lines correspond to the f/numbers on the lens' aperture scale.

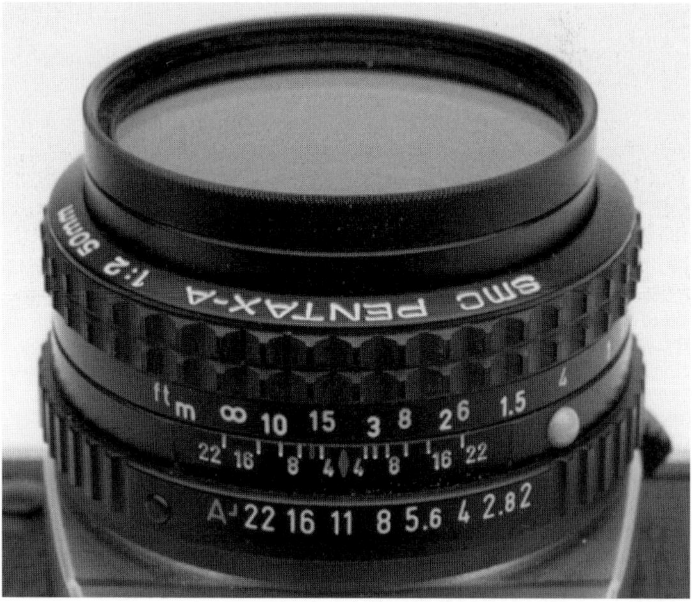

Use the lens' depth of field scale to determine how extensive the depth of field will be at a certain aperture.

To utilize the depth-of-field scale, first note the aperture that is set on the lens (the f/number opposite the aperture index). Locate the distance scale index that corresponds to the farthest object you want to appear sharp and align it with the left-hand line that

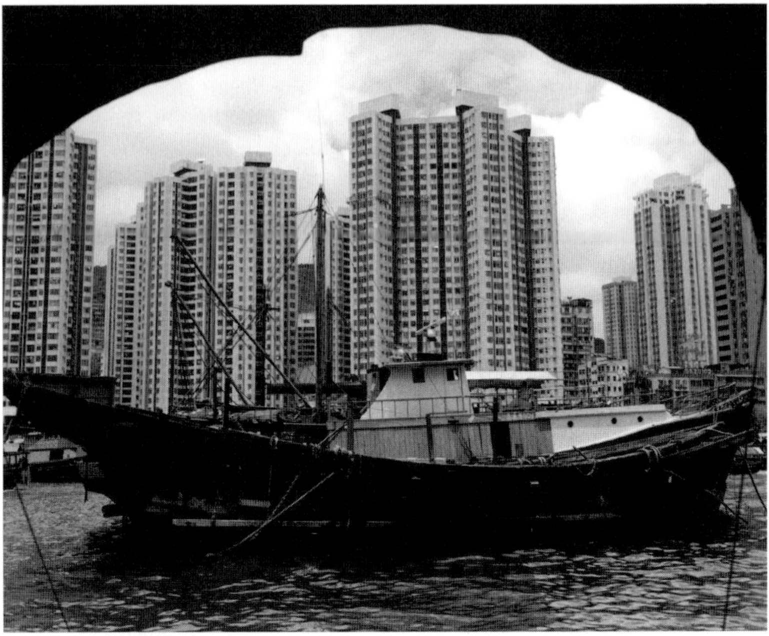

Be prepared! While we were touring the harbor, this shot presented itself, then was quickly gone. It was captured by predetermining the correct exposure and purposely selecting a small aperture to bring all the elements into sharp focus.

corresponds to the line of the set aperture. Now find the corresponding line on the right side of the depth-of-field scale. The distance that is opposite the right-hand line will be the closest distance that will be in focus at that aperture.

Hyperfocal Distance

Carrying the depth-of-field principle one step further, we can predetermine a point of focus that will bring close objects into sharp focus while insuring that objects at infinity are also in sharp focus. That point of focus is called the hyperfocal distance.

If a lens has a depth-of-field scale, setting the lens to the hyperfocal distance is easy. Determine the appropriate aperture, set infinity (on the lens' distance scale) opposite the f/stop selected (the one beyond the distance index on the depth-of-field scale), then observe the minimum distance that will be rendered sharply by finding the number on the distance scale that aligns with the duplicate f/stop on the near side of the focus point.

In other words, the hyperfocal distance is merely depth of field used so that the far point of focus includes infinity. When a novice understands depth of field and hyperfocal distance, he or she will realize that focusing using a focusing screen for many scenics is not only unnecessary, it wastes two-thirds of the available depth of field.

Depth of field and hyperfocal distance are influenced by two variables, f/stop and focal length. Most zoom lenses do not have depth-of-field scales on their barrels because it is impractical to place an infinitely variable chart there. A handy, easy-to-use pocket-sized calculator that computes depth of field for most lenses can be found in the *KODAK Pocket Photoguide.* Virtually every camera store stocks this necessary tool. It is filled with valuable data pertaining to most aspects of photography. No gadget bag should be without one. (For more information, contact Silver Pixel Press at 716-328-7800.)

Camera Care and Maintenance

Pride of ownership, protecting an investment, and preventing costly repairs are some good reasons for taking good care of your camera. The "shooter's" camera of today may be a "collectible" tomorrow, and the distinction between the two is often fuzzy. Many photographers still shoot with collectible cameras. A camera in "mint" condition is often worth twice the price of an identical model in poor cosmetic condition.

Many 20-year-old cameras that are still in operation have never been serviced. If a camera is properly used and carefully maintained, there is no reason to disassemble and clean it if no problem exists. Often there is little difference in cost between an actual repair and a tune-up or "CLA," Clean, Lube, and Adjust.

A camera is an instrument designed to be used, so problems can develop due to inactivity. Mechanically timed shutters (and self-timers) often become inaccurate because they are not used.

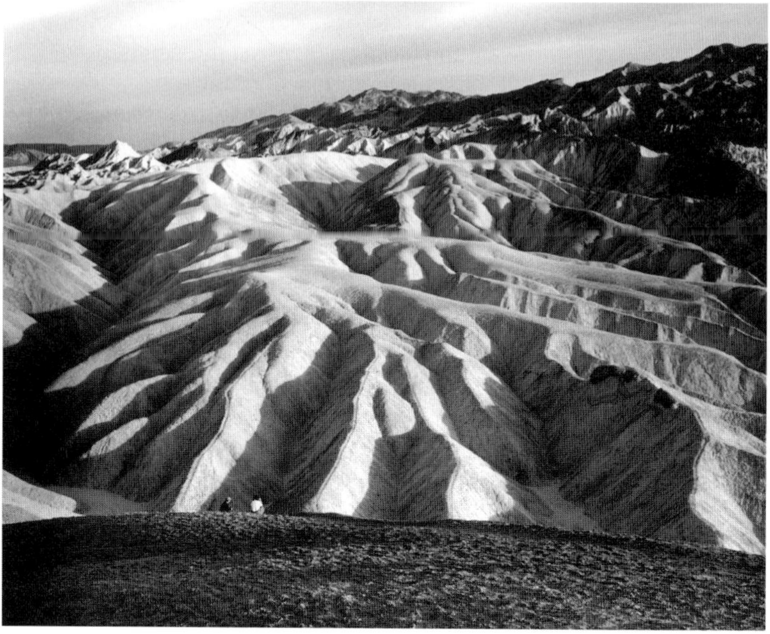

Late afternoon light casts shadows that add depth and dimension to a scene. The camera lens required to create this image should be clean, scratch-free, and well-maintained. The result? A super-sharp image.

This is especially true of the slower shutter speeds. Between rolls of film, take a moment to exercise all the seldom-used speeds. And don't leave the shutter cocked during periods of non-use!

Cameras can be damaged by extreme heat and/or humidity. A good rule of thumb is, if a storage site is too hot for a human being, it is too hot for camera gear. An automobile trunk is a poor place to stash equipment (for more than one reason). When using photo gear in potentially damaging conditions (dust, rain, etc.), plastic bags may offer some protection, but care must be taken not to trap humidity with the camera inside the plastic bag.

Equipment Care Kit

Every camera user should own an equipment care kit. Some people need a simple one, others may opt for a more elaborate setup. Below is a list of many items. You can decide for yourself how many of them you really need.

- ❑ A soft cloth (ideally an old cloth diaper or a lint-free dish towel) should be in every gadget bag and studio. The perfect camera cleaning cloth is smooth, lint free, and dust free and should be one that has been laundered multiple times. This cloth is usually used for general camera dusting and polishing. Use it on all non-glass surfaces. If spills or splashes occur, the faster the equipment is wiped off, the lower the risk of damage. The time wasted searching for a rag may be long enough for the liquid to migrate into delicate mechanisms.

- ❑ The ideal camera body cleaning brush is a new paintbrush that is approximately two inches (5 cm) wide. Select a brush with medium-soft natural bristles. The brush handle can be cut shorter to reduce weight and bulk in the gadget bag. Resist the urge to constantly feel the bristles; this loads them with dirt and oil. Brushes can be washed in laundry detergent, rinsed thoroughly, and used indefinitely.

The following camera care items are available from any good camera store:

Lens tissue: This is a valuable addition to your camera bag for many reasons. Lens tissue is comprised of long fibers that will not scratch lens coatings, deposit lint on the lens, or harm the surface you are trying to clean. Crumple a single piece into a loose ball for cleaning any camera surface. To clean a lens surface, with a circular motion start wiping the lens at the outer edge and gradually spiral into the center. Each piece of tissue is meant to be used once and then discarded. Facial tissues, shirt tails, and the backs of neckties can damage optics. *Do not use them on optical surfaces!*

Lens cleaning fluid: This should be used only when necessary and should never be applied directly to the lens surface. The fluid should be used to moisten the lens tissue, and then the moist tissue used to clean the surface. The lens should be dried with a dry lens tissue before the fluid has a chance to evaporate. Before trying lens cleaning fluid, though, breathe on the spot to be cleaned, then wipe with a dry lens tissue.

Canned air: Canned air does things that no other product can. Focusing screens and SLR mirrors cannot be cleaned in any other way. Touching them with even the softest unobtrusive material can damage them (there are certain cleaning procedures employed by specialized technicians, but they require skill and practice).

To use the pressurized air can, hold it level and tip the object to be cleaned. If an air can is tipped, its propellant can be emitted. This propellant will deposit an oily residue on the object it strikes. If it strikes a camera body it can be wiped away. However if it lands upon a shutter, prime-surface mirror, or plastic-surfaced focusing screen, costly repairs (or replacement) may be necessary.

This inert, ozone-safe, moisture-free air is useful for cleaning virtually any camera surface (care should be taken, though, because a strong, direct blast could possibly damage some shutter blades). All sorts of additional uses can be found in the photographic arena—lenses, darkroom items, and even the bottom of gadget bags may benefit from the use of a carefully directed blast of air. Negatives and transparency surfaces should be treated to a burst of air instead of (or before) being cleaned by other methods.

Canned air is marketed by many suppliers, comes in different sizes, and is available with different nozzle configurations. They are all good products, some better than others. Your requirements determine the best value.

Microfiber cloths: These cloths clean like no other product. The secret of their cleaning action is in the fabric employed and the density of the weave. Microfiber cloths whisk away fingerprints and other smudges more easily than lens tissue with or without lens cleaning fluid. They are so soft and gentle, they will not damage plastic filters or plastic eyeglasses (always blow dust, grit, or other solids off any optical surface before wiping it).

After much use these wonder cloths become ineffective, but that does not happen overnight. Care must be taken to keep them clean. When they slowly lose their effectiveness, they can be laundered. Hand-wash them in a mild detergent, rinse, and dry. They will work again, like they did when they were new.

Blower brushes: Blower brushes generate a gentle amount of air pressure, sometimes less than needed. And all blower brushes are not alike; some are more efficient than others. Before purchasing one, test it. If none are satisfactory, the answer may be another product. For instance, canned air comes in small containers. A container of canned air generates more cleaning pressure than the best blower brush.

Anti-static cloths: These cloths clean while eliminating static electricity. They should not be used to clean a dirty surface, but rather to polish a relatively clean one. They are intended for use on opaque surfaces and should *not* be used on glass. They are excellent for cleaning camera backs, film holders, and countless darkroom items.

Taking Care of Your Equipment

Always keep photographic equipment as clean as possible. If any foreign object lands on a camera, remove it as soon as possible. This is especially true of moisture. A camera's worst enemy is salt water. Salt-laden moisture continues to corrode working parts long after it enters. Most cameras that suffer salt-water damage are uneconomical to repair. When water enters a camera, the time lag between the occurrence and repair is critical. Get the camera to a repair facility as soon as possible!

Dust and dirt on a camera's surface for a short duration will probably do little or no damage. A careful cleaning immediately after a dusty shooting event will stop grime from migrating into the camera's interior. A camera that remains dirty for prolonged periods will eventually cause grief. Trouble may manifest itself in eventual damage to the mechanisms, difficult-to-remove specks in the viewfinder, a reduction in the resale value of the camera, and/or blemished film (irremovable spots or scratches).

A camera is a tool that is designed to be used. Unless it was obtained for its collector value it does no good being safely stored in a drawer. Each photographic event requires making intelligent choices. If a camera is used outdoors in a hurricane it will probably get wet, and wild horses running down a dusty canyon will probably cause dust to deposit on the camera that captured the event. However, sometimes photographers fear more for their equipment than their own lives!

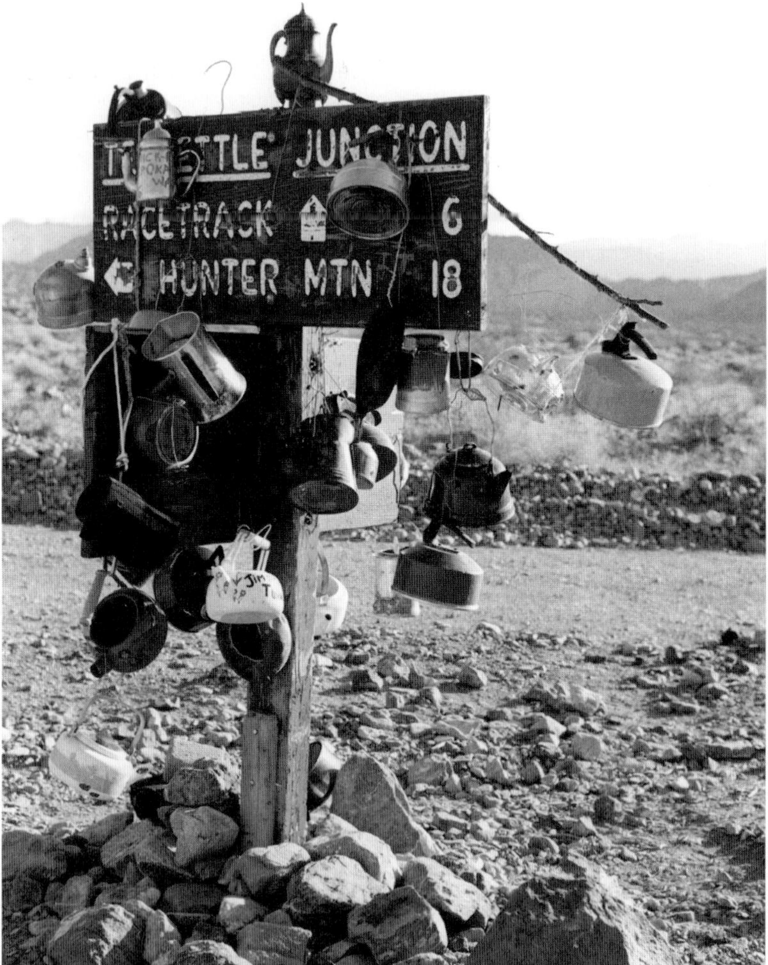

Humor is everywhere, even in the middle of nowhere. This junction is inaccessible at times and often passable only in 4-wheel-drive vehicles. Heat and dust are no excuse for missing a good shot, but after a dusty shooting session, be sure to clean your camera thoroughly.

The prepared photographer can take precautions. The entire gadget bag can be put into a large plastic bag for an entire dusty Jeep ride, then pictures can be taken after the dust settles. A few raindrops can be wiped from the camera's surface after the shot has been made.

Some photographers pamper their equipment. Some treat camera gear roughly. Some people purchase used, cosmetically inferior cameras for use in situations that could be hazardous to their equipment. How your equipment is treated is up to you. Probably a middle-of-the-road approach is best.

Spotmatic Series

The Asahi Pentax Spotmatics were some of the most popular single-lens-reflex (SLR) cameras ever offered for sale by a camera manufacturer. The line had a long and successful run—the first Spot-Matic prototype was unveiled in 1960, and the final Spotmatic (the Spotmatic F) was introduced in 1974.

The Spotmatic was an evolutionary camera; model changes usually consisted of minor variations. Understanding the mechanics of any model will quickly allow the user to understand all the Spotmatics. First, we will study the Spotmatic chronology. Then, we will examine the data required to understand the most complicated Spotmatic.

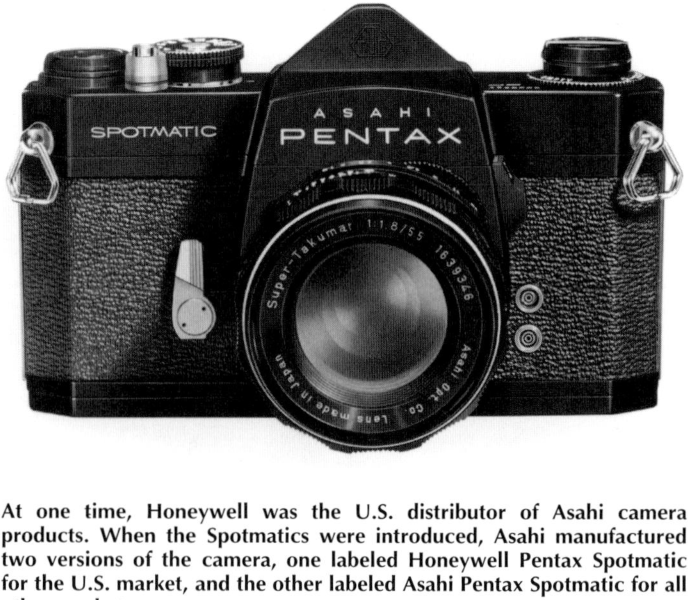

At one time, Honeywell was the U.S. distributor of Asahi camera products. When the Spotmatics were introduced, Asahi manufactured two versions of the camera, one labeled Honeywell Pentax Spotmatic for the U.S. market, and the other labeled Asahi Pentax Spotmatic for all other markets.

Note: During the Spotmatic era, Honeywell was the supplier of Asahi products in the United States. It is common practice in the photographic industry to use the name "Honeywell," but the correct name is actually "The Denver Division of Minneapolis-Honeywell Regulator Company." The name "Honeywell" appears on products imported by them; an identical model sporting the name "Asahi" means that it was manufactured for sale outside the U.S. Fortunately, model designations were identical worldwide.

Asahi/Honeywell Pentax Spotmatic Specifications

Type:	35mm (24 x 36mm format), single-lens-reflex
Lens Mount:	Pentax-type screw mount (42mm)
Viewfinder:	Pentaprism finder with microprism Fresnel focusing screen; 0.88x magnification with 50mm lens; approximately life size with 55mm lens
Shutter:	Focal plane shutter
Shutter Speeds:	1/1000 second to 1 second, plus bulb (B)
Film Advance:	Single-stroke advance lever; 10° stand-off position, 160° advancing angle
Film Rewind:	Film rewind knob with folding rapid-rewind crank
Frame Counter:	Additive; automatic resetting
Exposure Meter:	Behind-the-lens meter
Film Speed Range:	ISO 20 to 1600
Flash Synchronization:	Focal plane at all speeds; X sync of 1/60 second
Power Source:	Originally took one E400N-type battery or equivalent; now takes WeinCell MRB400.
Dimensions:	3.4 D x 3.6 H x 5.6″W (88 x 92 x 143 mm)
Weight:	22 oz. (621 g)

Spotmatic Chronology

Spot-Matic
Introduced 1960

The Spot-Matic prototype was introduced in 1960 in Cologne, Germany, at Photokina, the world's largest photography show. Although the prototype was never offered for sale, it fascinated the photographic world. It contained a behind-the-lens spot meter, the source of its name. When the first production model was introduced, the hyphen was dropped, and the spot meter was replaced with two cells that yielded an average meter reading.

Spotmatic (SP)
Introduced 1964

The complete name of this camera model is either *Asahi Pentax Spotmatic* or *Honeywell Pentax Spotmatic,* depending upon where the camera was sold. The Asahi Pentax Spotmatic, sold in markets outside the U.S. also has "SP" printed on its top plate, below the serial number.

Its outward appearance resembles previous Asahi cameras, but its working mechanisms were completely redesigned. There were also some exterior design modifications, mainly the more robust lens mount.

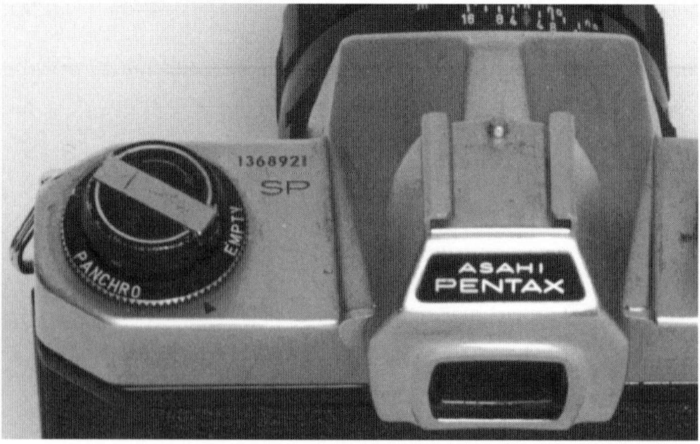

Asahi Pentax Spotmatics have "SP" printed on their top plate, while the Honeywell models do not.

Pentax SL
Introduced 1968
The Pentax SL is identical to the Spotmatic except it does not contain a light meter and therefore is a few ounces lighter. It requires no battery. Technically it is not a Spotmatic, but since all the functions, controls, operational procedures (except meter functions), and its appearance are classic Spotmatic, we've included it here. Asahi produced this "meter-less Spotmatic" so they could enter the marketplace with a lower-priced SLR.

Spotmatic II (SP II)
Introduced 1971
The one easily identifiable new feature of the SP II is its hot shoe. Also, the upper limit of the light meter sensitivity range was increased from ASA/ISO 1600 to 3200. These are the only external differences between the Spotmatic and the Spotmatic II.

Spotmatic IIa (SP IIa)
Introduced 1972
Designed for the American market, the Honeywell Pentax Spotmatic IIa never caught on. It was identical to the Spotmatic II, but with one additional feature—on its face, just below the rewind knob, is a flash sensor. When used in conjunction with a dedicated Honeywell electronic flash, this sensor would automatically control exposure. Automatic flash units and TTL (Through-the-Lens) flash metering were soon to arrive; unfortunately, the IIa offered too little, too late.

Spotmatic SP 500
Introduced 1971
The SP 500 is like the original Spotmatic, but in order to compete in a lower-priced category, it was designed with a top shutter speed of only 1/500 second and does not include a self-timer.

Spotmatic SP 1000
Introduced 1974
The SP 1000 is identical to the SP 500, but its top shutter speed is 1/1000 second.

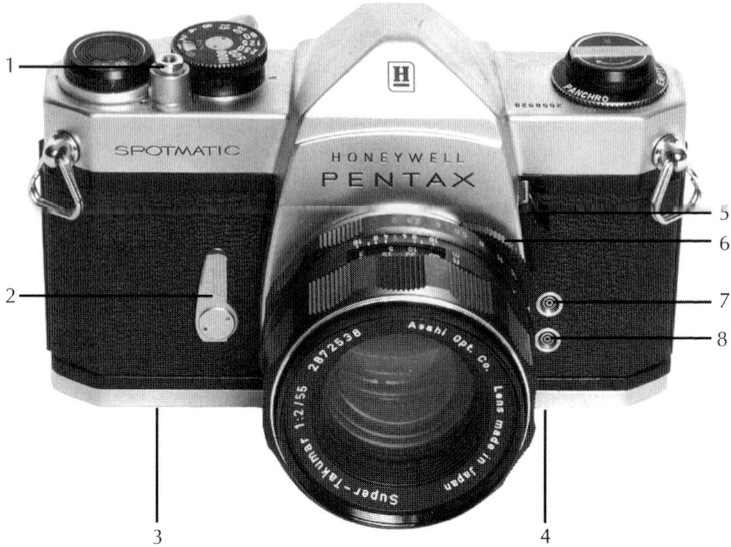

Honeywell Pentax Spotmatic
Shown are the features common to the Spotmatic, Spotmatic II, IIa, F, SP 500, SP 1000, and Pentax SL

1. **Shutter release button (F has locking collar surrounding it)**
2. **Self-timer lever (none on SP 500 and SP 1000)**
3. **Rewind button (on base of camera)**
4. **Battery cover (on base of camera; none on SL)**
5. **Meter on/off switch (none on SL)/Depth-of-field preview lever (on F only)**
6. **Depth-of-field preview lever (on Super Takumar and most SMC Takumar lenses)**
7. **FP flash sync terminal**
8. **X flash sync terminal**

Spotmatic F (SPF)
Introduced 1974

The final camera in the Spotmatic line is identical to the Spotmatic II but includes a shutter release lock and one additional feature: When used with most Super Multi-Coated Takumar lenses, meter readings are taken with the lens at full aperture. Previous models measured light correctly only after the lens was stopped down. Unlike the other Spotmatics, this model originally took a PX625 (or equivalent) battery; now it must take a WeinCell MRB625.

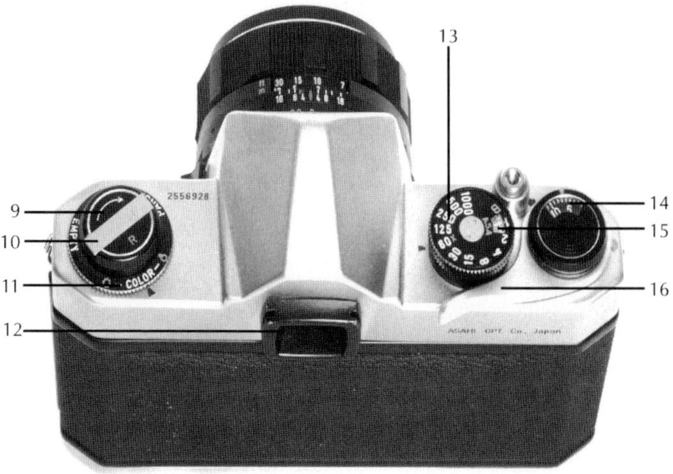

9. **Rewind knob**
10. **Rewind crank**
11. **Film type reminder dial**
12. **Viewfinder eyepiece**
13. **Shutter speed dial**
14. **Frame counter**
15. **ASA/ISO film speed window (none on SL)**
16. **Rapid wind film advance lever**

Spotmatic Motor Drive

This is not a camera, per se, but rather a specially designed model of the standard Pentax camera. The Pentax Spotmatic had a motor-drive version, as did the Spotmatic II and Spotmatic F.

It is easy to identify a Spotmatic that is capable of being motor driven because the words "Motor Drive" are imprinted on its face. Other than the drive functions, all functions are identical to the rest of the cameras of that particular model run. A Spotmatic F Motor Drive camera, for example, would have all the Spotmatic F characteristics, plus the "Motor Drive" nameplate.

Spotmatic Accessories

Asahi and other manufacturers supplied accessories for the Spotmatic cameras. Some of these accessories fit other Asahi cameras as well. See the *Accessories* chapter for specific details.

Using the Spotmatic Cameras

Battery Installation and Testing

Before operating the camera, determine that the correct battery is installed in the camera's battery chamber. Currently, you will need to use the WeinCell MRB400 for all Spotmatics except the F, which takes the WeinCell MRB625. Because the Pentax SL has no meter, no battery is required. (See page 15 for more information on batteries.)

The battery chamber is located on the camera's base; it is clearly marked "battery." Unscrew the battery chamber cover with a coin. Insert the new battery, following the polarity markings on the chamber.

Batteries should never be stored in a camera for a prolonged time, as they may deteriorate. When batteries deteriorate there is a chemical reaction, which may cause the battery chamber cover to lock in place (this is especially possible in Spotmatics). Brute force will only damage the soft brass cover.

To test the battery, set the shutter speed dial to B. Position the ASA/ISO dial to "100." Turn the meter switch to "on." While looking through the viewfinder, observe the meter needle. If the battery is satisfactory, the needle will drop rapidly. If it does not, replace the battery.

Loading Film

Open the camera back by pulling the rewind knob up until the back springs open. Load the camera in the conventional manner and close the door. (See page 19 for complete instructions on loading film.)

Advancing Film and Cocking the Shutter

Move the film advance lever through an arc of 160° to advance the film one frame and cock the shutter. The Spotmatics contain a built-in mechanism that prevents double exposures from being made accidentally and also prevents you from advancing the film past an unexposed frame.

Note: Spotmatics do not have a multiple-exposure feature as other Pentax models do.

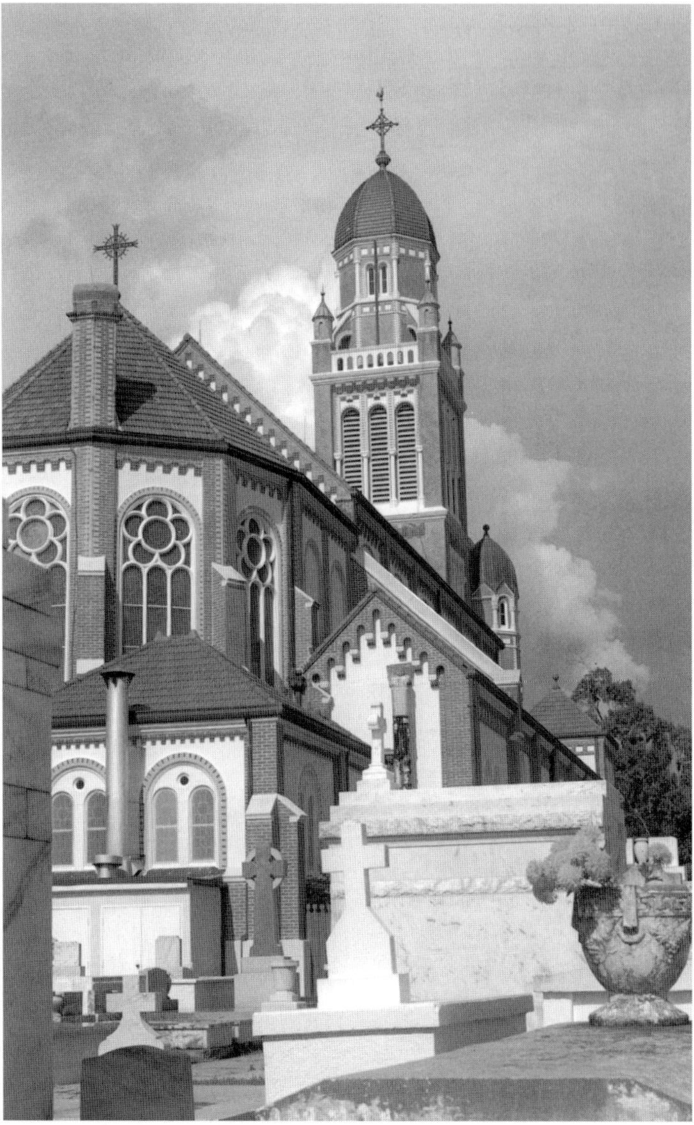

When you're traveling, take an assortment of film with you. High-speed films open up possibilities of taking pictures after dark and inside buildings. Slower-speed films are ideal for outdoor shooting in bright locations.

Setting the Film Speed

Lift the outer ring of the shutter speed dial. Rotate it to set the desired film speed so it aligns with the red index by the ASA/ISO film speed window.

Note: When Spotmatics were being manufactured, a film's sensitivity to light was rated in many parts of the world (including the U.S.) using a numerical rating called ASA. Today, we use a worldwide standard called ISO. The numerical value of a film's sensitivity is the same in both systems.

Surrounding the rewind knob is the film type reminder dial. It is merely a dial that you can set to remind yourself what type of film, if any, is in the camera. It has no functional purpose; its use is strictly optional.

Focusing

Spotmatic cameras are made with a ground glass focusing screen with a central microprism circle. This focusing device is the best universal focusing system found in any manually focused camera. Split-image rangefinders work well in bright light, and ground glass focusing is suitable with long telephoto lenses, but the best compromise is the microprism. It works under all the above conditions, and more.

The Spotmatic's ground glass viewfinder screen is made brighter by a light-amplification screen called a Fresnel lens. In the center of the finder is a circular spot, which is the microprism. When a subject is in focus, it appears sharp and perfectly clear. When the subject is not in focus, the microprism breaks up and images appear as glittering, disturbing dots. It is easy to focus with the Spotmatic—place the subject in the viewfinder's center circle and then turn the lens' focusing ring until the image becomes sharp on the microprism grid and surrounding fine-focusing collar.

Shutter Speed Dial

Rotate the shutter speed dial to select the desired shutter speed. The numbers from 2 to 1000 indicate fractions of a second; for example, "2" means 1/2 second, "1000" means 1/1000 second. The "1" on the shutter speed dial represents one full second.

"B" stands for "bulb," which allows exposures longer than one second. In the B position the photographer must determine the length of exposure by using a separate timing device, such as a clock or a stopwatch.

The index mark to which shutter speeds are set resembles a blunted arrowhead. When this index is red, the shutter speed-film speed combination is beyond the light meter's sensitivity range.

Shutter Release

The shutter release button is located between the shutter speed dial and the film advance lever. The shutter must be cocked before the shutter will release. While holding the camera steady, depress the shutter release button smoothly. A carefully tripped release helps reduce the chance of camera shake.

When the shutter is released, the meter/depth-of-field switch will automatically turn off, and the aperture will reopen to its maximum setting. Now the viewfinder image will be at its brightest, and the film advance lever can be recocked.

Light Meter Activation and Depth-of-Field Preview

All Spotmatic cameras except the SL have a switch labeled "SW" located on the left shoulder of the mirror box, between the lens and the camera's body. This switch performs two functions (only

All Spotmatic models (excluding the SL) have a meter on/off switch, which doubles as a depth-of-field preview switch. On the Spotmatic F, this switch acts only as depth-of-field preview lever; its meter is on as long as a lens is mounted, the lens cap is removed, and a good battery is installed.

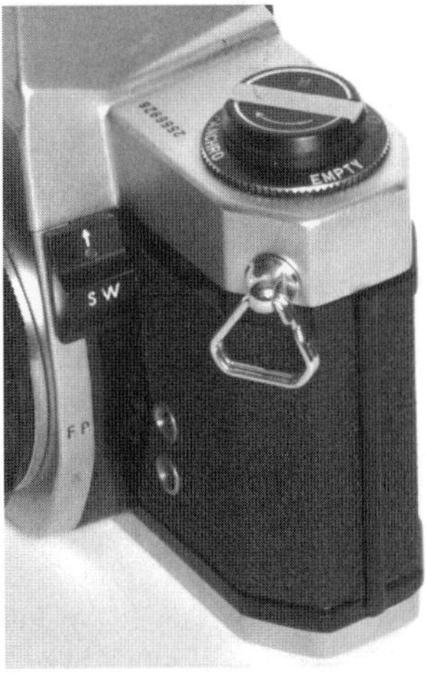

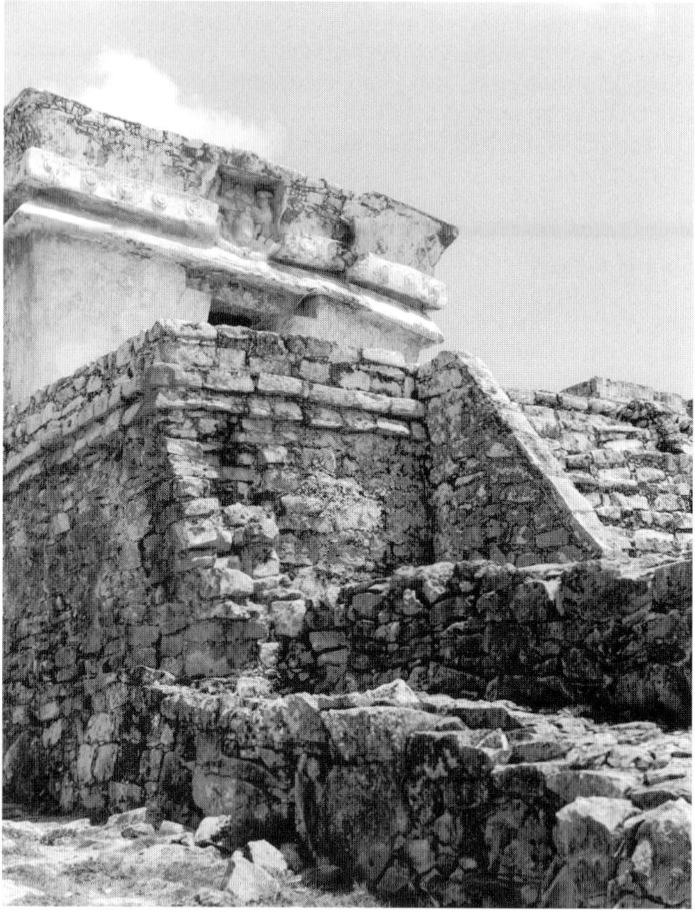

Sidelighting creates contrast and texture, two of the major elements in this photo. Frontal lighting would have reduced the three-dimensional effect, losing much of the structure's character.

one on the Spotmatic F)—depth-of-field preview and light meter activation. (It serves only as a depth-of-field preview switch on the F.) The meter circuit is turned on by pushing up on the switch. A small window at the top of the switch turns red when the meter is activated.

Activating this switch not only turns on the meter, but causes the lens to stop down to the value indicated on the lens' aperture ring. The farther the lens is stopped down, the darker the image becomes in the viewfinder. This is essential in determining depth of field, but a darkened viewfinder can make composition difficult. Therefore, to use this switch for light meter activation, focus and compose *before* you determine exposure. (See "Setting Exposure" below.) When the shutter is tripped, this switch automatically returns to the "off" position.

This is the correct procedure for normal, speedy operation. However, there are situations that call for deviation. After a meter reading has been taken, you can manually turn the switch off by pushing it down to its original position. This way, exposure determination can precede other considerations.

With the Spotmatic F, the light meter is on when a lens is mounted, the lens cap is removed, and an adequately powered battery is installed. The only way to turn the meter off is to remove the lens or the battery. Placing the lens cap on reduces the power draw to almost zero, but it does not turn the meter off.

Note: Many Spotmatic F users were upset by this lack of an on/off switch, but it hasn't had an adverse effect on battery replacement. If the lens is capped when the camera is not in use, the Spotmatic F requires battery replacement at approximately the same rate as Spotmatics that contain a meter switch.

Super Takumar and most SMC Takumar lenses (which were designed to operate with Spotmatics) are equipped with a switch that allows the lens to be stopped down. This switch, or semi-circular lever, is located on the lens ring closest to the camera body. It can be switched to the "AUTO" or "MAN" (Manual) position. For simple operation, keep the lens switch to the "AUTO" position. If left in the "MAN" position, the automatic diaphragm is disengaged, resulting in a darkened viewfinder at most working apertures.

Setting Exposure

With the meter on, select an appropriate shutter speed for your photo—for example, one that has the proper action-stopping ability or will yield the ideal depth of field.

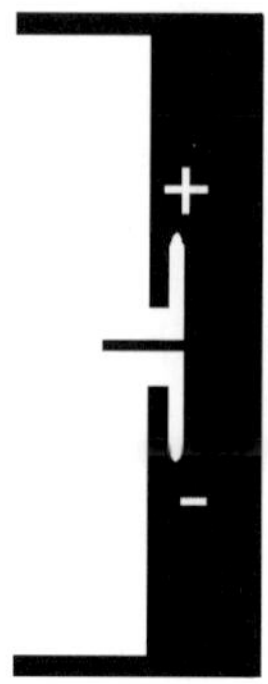

If the needle on the Spotmatic's meter display points up to the +, overexposure is indicated, if it points down to the –, underexposure will result. To follow the meter's recommended exposure setting, adjust the aperture and shutter speed until the needle is aligned midway between the symbols. The Pentax K1000 and KM cameras also have this meter display.

Next, look through your viewfinder. On the right border is a cut-out segment that has a "+" on the top and a "–" on the bottom. To match the meter's recommended exposure setting, turn the aperture ring or shutter speed dial until the meter needle is pointing horizontally, centered precisely in the channel.

A lens can be set anywhere throughout its aperture range; partial stops are often required for precise exposure control. You can also turn the shutter speed dial to adjust the exposure, but the dial can be set only on the exact speed detents.

Setting exposure is the same with the Spotmatic F, but the meter does not need to be switched on as it is automatically activated with a lens mounted and batteries installed.

Self-Timer

The large lever located on the left side of the camera's face (as you look at the front of the camera) is the self-timer. It creates a delay between the time the release button is tripped and the time the shutter opens. The delay can vary anywhere from 5 to 12 seconds depending on whether the lever is fully or partially cocked. The self-timer release button, which must be pressed to activate the timing mechanism, is hidden by the top of the self-timer lever when it is in the "stored" position. It is visible only when the lever has been cocked (rotated in a downward arc).

To take a self-timed photograph, cock the shutter, cock the self-timer lever, and press the now-revealed self-timer button. The photo will be taken after the timer runs down. The shutter release is not involved in taking self-timed exposures.

If the self-timer lever has been cocked and you wish to take a non-delayed photograph, you can press the shutter release and it will ignore the timer. The self-timer button can be pressed at a later time.

Basic Flash Operation

Flash bulbs were still being used back when Spotmatics were being produced. Since flash bulbs and electronic flash units have radically different synchronization requirements, there are two PC flash terminals ("X" and "FP") on the left face of the camera.

Electronic flash units must be connected to the X terminal. (FP is for flash bulb use.) If flash contact is being achieved through a flash cord, it must be plugged into the X terminal, clearly marked on the side of the mirror housing wall. Some Spotmatics (II, IIa, and F) have a built-in accessory hot shoe, which is an X sync outlet.

To achieve proper flash synchronization, the shutter must be set to a compatible speed. Spotmatic cameras will synchronize with electronic flash at 1/60 second or slower (down to 1 second). As a reminder of the camera's sync speed, 1/60 second is marked with a small X on the shutter speed dial.

Today, flash bulbs are all but extinct, and even if obtainable, they are too costly for everyday use. For information purposes only, flash bulb sync speeds are listed below.

"FP" type bulbs:	1/1000, 1/500, 1/250, 1/125, and 1/60 second
"F" type bulbs:	1/15, 1/8, 1/4, 1/2, and 1 second
"M" type bulbs:	1/8, 1/4, 1/2, and 1 second

Pentax K Series

In 1975, Asahi introduced several cameras to its line—the K2, KM, and KX models. The K1000 was introduced the following year, and the K2 DMD a short time later. (Information on the K1000 is in another *Magic Lantern Guide*.) As suggested by the models' designations, these cameras use Pentax K-mount (bayonet-type) lenses.

Note: For all practical purposes, the K-series cameras signaled the end of the screw-mount lens era. Other manufacturers continued to produce cameras that utilized screw-mount lenses, but their popularity rapidly declined. See the chapter *Asahi/Pentax Lenses* for more information.

For a camera company to bring four new cameras to the marketplace in such a short time was a brave—and relatively unheard of—move. The bayonet-mount cameras were eventually well received, and a new era in SLR photography began.

Each of the K-series cameras had its own place in the family; at the top of the line was the K2. We will examine it first, look at its features, discuss how it operates, and describe how it differs from its relatives. For more in-depth information on operating these cameras, please see the chapter *Using Your Pentax Classic Camera.*

Asahi Pentax K2 Specifications

Introduced: 1975

Type: 35mm (24 x 36mm format), single-lens-reflex

Lens Mount: Asahi Pentax K bayonet mount

Viewfinder: Pentaprism finder. 0.88x magnification with 50mm lens. Life-size with 55mm lens. Field of view is 95%.

Focusing Screen: Some K2s were equipped with microprism focusing screens, others with split-image focusing screens.

Shutter:	Vertically traveling, metal blade, electronic focal plane shutter
Shutter Speeds:	
Manual Electronic:	8, 4, 2, 1, 1/2, 1/4, 1/8, 1/15, 1/30, 1/60, 1/125, 1/250, 1/500, 1/1000 second
Manual Mechanical:	B and 1/125 second
Automatic Electronic:	Stepless between 8 seconds and 1/1000 second
Reflex Mirror:	Instant-return type, with mirror lock-up lever and vibration-reducing shock absorbers
Film Advance:	Single-stroke lever; 25° stand-off position; 130° advance angle
Film Rewind:	Rapid-rewind crank
Frame Counter:	Additive; automatic reset
Exposure Meter:	Silicon-Photo-Diode cell. In Automatic mode, Aperture-Preferred (Aperture-Priority) metering. In Manual mode, match-needle metering. In either mode, full-aperture metering with measurement of the entire ground-glass area, but biased for the central portion. Full-information viewfinder.
Exposure Compensation:	1/4x, 1/2x, 1x, 2x, and 4x (–2, –1, 0, +1, +2 stops)
Self-Timer:	Built-in self-timer with interrupt capability. Variable delay time from 5 to 9 seconds.
Flash Synchronization:	FP and X—FP through terminal on camera body; X through terminal on camera body or hot shoe. X sync speed = 1/125 second.
Power Source:	Two 1.5v S76-type batteries, or equivalent
Dimensions with 50mm lens:	3.7 D x 3.6 H x 5.7″W (94 x 92 x 144 mm)
Weight:	Body only: 24.2 oz. (680 g). Body with 50mm f/1.4 lens: 33.7 oz. (946 g)

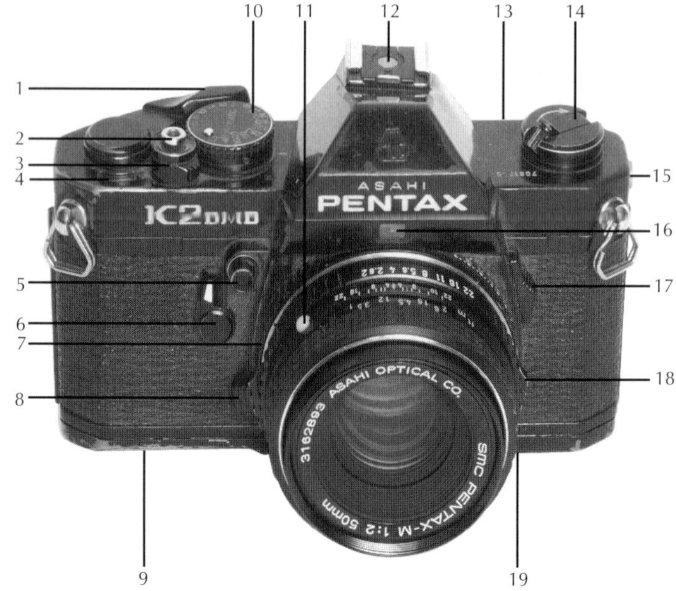

Asahi Pentax K2 DMD

The Pentax K2 DMD camera (pictured) is virtually identical to the K2. Exceptions are noted.

1. **Film advance lever**
2. **Shutter release**
3. **Shutter release lock**
4. **Frame counter**
5. **Depth-of-field preview button**
6. **Self-timer**
7. **Exposure compensation scale**
8. **Lens release**
9. **Rewind button (on base of camera)**
10. **Shutter speed dial**
11. **Lens mounting guide**
12. **X sync accessory shoe**
13. **Battery check button and light (on back of camera)**
14. **Rewind crank**
15. **FP and X flash sync terminals**
16. **Aperture readout window (K2 DMD only)**
17. **Mirror lock-up and exposure lock lever (only locks mirror up on K2)**
18. **ASA/ISO film speed ring and lever**
19. **Battery compartment (on base of camera)**

Using the Pentax K2

Battery Installation and Testing

The Pentax K2 requires two S76-type batteries or the equivalent.

Although lithium or alkaline batteries can also be used with the Pentax K2, we recommend silver-oxide batteries because they are long lived, and they outperform other batteries in cold temperatures.

The battery holders on the K-series cameras are marked with a polarity diagram for easy installation. The battery test button and the battery check light are located on the back of the camera between the rewind knob and viewfinder. To test the batteries' condition, press the test button. If the light comes on, battery power is sufficient; if not, they should be replaced.

If the batteries fail and you have no replacement cells handy, the camera can be used manually with shutter speeds of "B" or 1/125 second. When the batteries cannot power the light meter, you must determine exposure values using a hand-held meter, exposure chart, or your best guesstimate.

Advancing Film

The film advance lever stores in a position that is virtually flush with the camera's top edge. It has a stand-off position of 25° for rapid film advancement, which can be used even when you are not looking at the lever. The advance lever can be placed in either the cocked or "at-rest" position at any time.

To advance the film, move the film advance lever through an arc of 130°. A single stroke advances the film to the next frame. The camera has a built-in device that prevents unintentional double exposures.

When a photographer is in tune with his or her camera, he or she knows when everything feels "right." If film advancement feels rough, stiff, or unusual, stop! If you force the advance lever, you may rip the film or pull its end out of the cassette. At the first indication that film advancement is not going smoothly, find out why. Usually rewinding the film is the best solution.

Setting the Film Speed

The K2's film speed scale is located on a band surrounding the lens mount. First set the exposure compensation scale on the right side of the lens mount (as you hold the camera) to 1x. To set the film speed, depress the locking lever located on the left side of the lens mount at five o'clock, and turn the ISO ring until the desired film speed is opposite the orange index mark.

Memo Holder

The camera back contains a memo holder that is conveniently sized to hold a film box end. Since the box end includes both film type and the number of exposures on the roll, it is a useful reminder, and often a lifesaver for photographers who change film types often or who leave a partially exposed roll of film in the camera.

Focusing Screens

The Pentax K2 came equipped with either a microprism or split-image focusing screen. These focusing screens are interchangeable but require a competent repair technician to do the job properly. Today, replacement screens for K2 cameras are difficult to locate. (See page 31 for more information on focusing.)

Shutter Speed Dial

The shutter speed dial allows the photographer to select his or her choice of shutter speeds from B to 1/1000 second. "B" stands for "bulb"; it keeps the shutter open as long as the shutter release button is depressed. The numbers between 1 and B (2, 4, and 8) refer to full seconds. The numbers between 1 and Automatic represent fractions of a second (2=1/2 second, 60=1/60 second, etc.). 1/125 is the fastest shutter speed that can be used to synchronize with electronic flash.

Shutter Release Lock

Surrounding the shutter release button is the shutter release lock lever. To prevent the shutter from being released accidentally, lock the shutter button by turning the locking lever until the "L" becomes visible.

Light Meter Activation

The light meter is switched on by cocking the shutter and pressing the shutter release partway. However, the film advance lever's position has an effect on meter activation as well. If the film advance lever is flush with the camera body, the light meter is active only if the shutter release button is pressed partway. It will shut off when your finger is lifted off the shutter release.

If the film advance lever is in its stand-off position and the shutter release is pressed partway, the meter will remain on until the film advance lever is returned to its flush position.

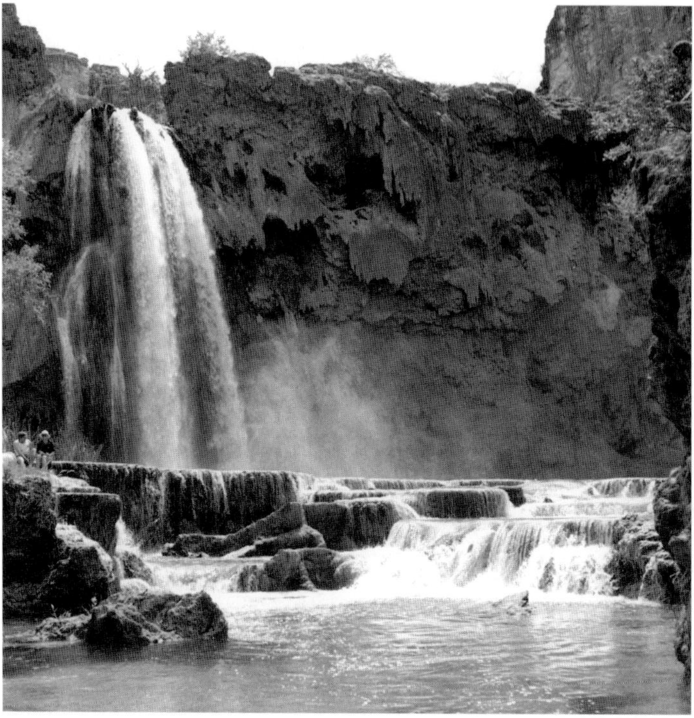

When photographing waterfalls, numerous effects can be achieved just by changing the shutter speed. Fast speeds tend to freeze the movement of the water, and slow speeds will blur it, creating the impression of motion.

Viewfinder Exposure Data

The light meter data scale is located along the right side of the focusing screen in the viewfinder. There are two needles—black and blue-green—and a scale of shutter speed numbers. The black needle points to the shutter speed recommended by the camera's meter in both Automatic and Manual mode. The blue-green needle points to "AUTO" if the camera is in Automatic mode, or to the manually selected shutter speed if the camera is in Manual mode. In conjunction with this, you'll find a scale of shutter speeds: the black numbers refer to fractions of a second and the white numbers refer to full seconds.

The K2's viewfinder display has two needles that help you determine correct exposure. The black needle indicates the shutter speed recommended by the meter at the set aperture, and the blue-green needle points to the selected shutter speed (in Manual mode) or "AUTO" (in Automatic mode). Here, the camera is in Automatic mode and has set a shutter speed of 1/250 second.

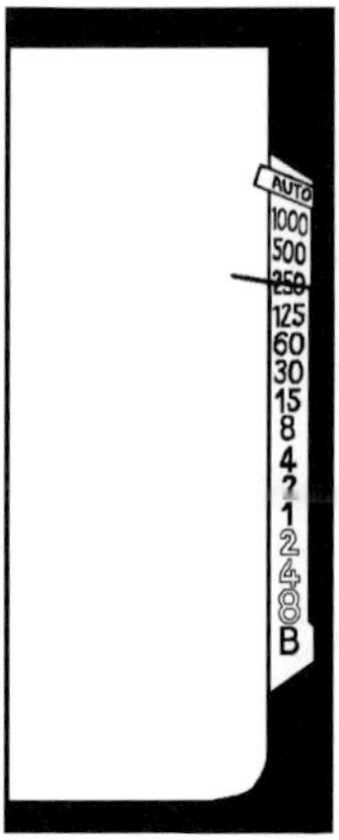

Automatic Exposure Control

Today, what was once called Automatic mode is now called Aperture-Preferred or Aperture-Priority mode. In this mode, the photographer selects the aperture and the camera selects the corresponding shutter speed.

To use Automatic mode, first set the shutter speed dial to "Automatic." Advance the film to cock the shutter, and depress the shutter release button partway to activate the meter. Use the data in the viewfinder to guide you in setting the desired exposure.

Setting the shutter speed dial to "Automatic" sends the viewfinder's blue-green needle to "AUTO." When the meter is activated, the black needle points to the shutter speed selected by the camera's metering system, taking into account the current aperture selected. If the shutter speed will not achieve the effect you desire, you can adjust the aperture setting until the appropriate shutter speed is selected by the camera.

***Caution**: If the camera is in Automatic mode and the shutter is tripped while the lens cap is in place, the camera will seem to "jam." To clear the system, simply turn the shutter speed dial to any other shutter speed.*

Manual Exposure Control

Even in Manual mode, the camera's light meter will still indicate what its exposure recommendations are. You have more control in Manual mode, but you sacrifice operating speed.

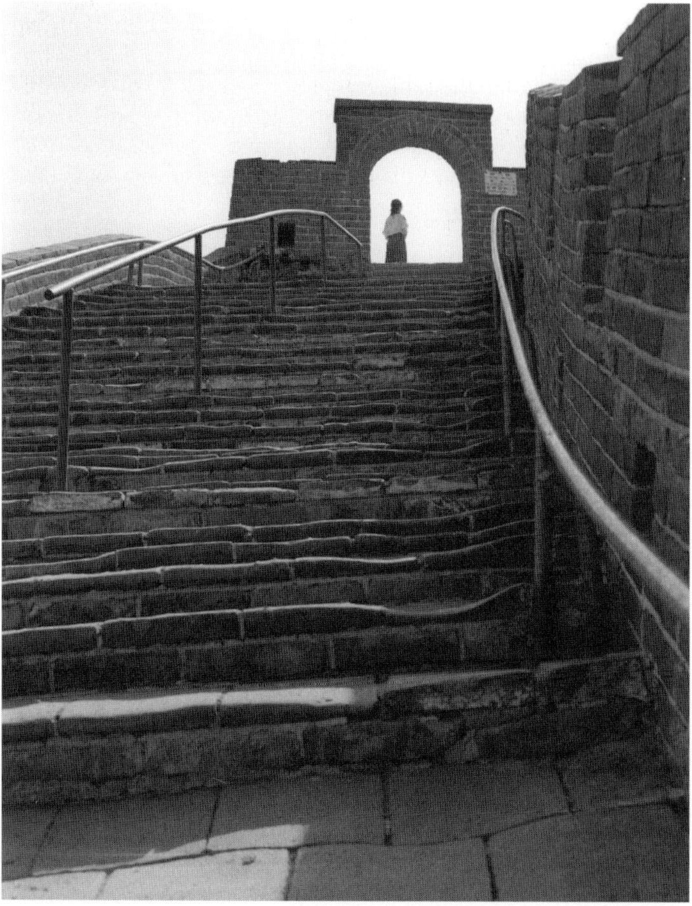

Backlighting was used to give China's Great Wall some depth and dimension. Use Manual mode to set the proper exposure for such situations. A highlight and a shadow reading told me this scene was barely within the film's contrast range.

To use the K2 in Manual mode, first select the desired shutter speed, then press the shutter release partway to activate the light meter, and look at the viewfinder display. The blue-green needle points to the shutter speed you selected and the black needle indicates the shutter speed recommended by the camera's metering system. If you want to follow the meter's recommendation, turn either the aperture control ring or the shutter speed dial until the two needles point to the same number. However, if you follow the meter's recommendation, you have not accomplished anything that you couldn't have done by using Automatic mode. Manual exposure mode is best used to isolate or accentuate a subject, or to compensate or otherwise customize a meter reading for creative effect.

Exposure Compensation

The exposure compensation scale is located near the lens mount, by the self-timer lever. The scale allows you to intentionally over- or underexpose your film when the camera is in Automatic exposure mode. For normal exposure settings, the scale should be set at 1x. 2x will double the amount of light that reaches the film, and 4x will quadruple the amount of light—both may cause overexposure. Conversely, 1/2x reduces light transmission by half, and 1/4x yields a quarter of the light, causing possible underexposure.

Exposure can also be adjusted simply by adjusting the shutter speed or aperture. You can double the quantity of light reaching the film by opening the aperture up one stop or slowing the shutter speed down by a stop.

Exposure compensation sounds simple, but it takes time to accurately determine how much compensation is needed. Many experienced photographers prefer to use an alternate metering method when they suspect that an automatic setting will not produce the desired results.

Multiple Exposures

To make multiple exposures on the same frame of film, make the first exposure in the conventional way. Then remove all the slack from the film in the cassette by turning the rewind knob in the direction of its arrow. When the film is tightly wrapped around its core, depress the rewind button and wind the film advance lever once. This cocks the shutter without advancing the film. Now make the second exposure. A tripod is often helpful when taking multiple exposures as it helps control the subject's placement within the frame.

***Caution**: The Pentax K2 has a tripod screw socket that allows a screw up to 5.5 mm (approximately 1/5 inch) long to be inserted.*

Be advised that a screw that is any longer can severely damage the camera.

Any number of exposures can be made on top of previous exposures using this method. Some skill and practice is required to achieve perfectly balanced multiple exposures. Depending on the subject placement and lighting of each exposure, some exposure compensation may be required. This technique is best learned by practicing before the actual need arises.

After you have finished taking the last exposure for the frame, we suggest that you make one blank frame. Trip the shutter with it set to a fast speed and with the lens cap firmly in place. This will prevent subsequent frames from overlapping onto your multiple exposure, since registration is not always exact.

Mirror Lock-up Lever

Under normal picture-taking situations, when the shutter is tripped, the reflex mirror swings up out of the way during the instant of exposure, then returns to its normal position. This action, called "mirror bounce," introduces a slight amount of camera movement. Normally this small amount of vibration does not affect the photo, however in high-magnification photography or when shooting at slower shutter speeds, it may introduce enough vibration to show up in the image. When photographing with microscopes, telescopes, long telephoto lenses, and macro lenses, it may be advisable to eliminate mirror bounce.

The mirror lock-up lever is located on the left side of the lens mount (as you hold the camera in the shooting position). Push the lever up to lock up the mirror. With the mirror locked, the only internal vibration comes from the shutter's movement, and that is minimal.

When the mirror is locked, light cannot enter the viewfinder through the lens. Therefore, you must view and frame the image before the mirror is locked up. Also, because light is likewise restricted from the metering system, exposure settings must be determined in advance. This lever doubles as an exposure lock lever on the K2 DMD. (See page 70 for more information.)

The photographer who goes to these lengths to reduce internal vibrations is also naturally concerned with the sources of external vibrations. The sturdiest possible camera support should be used and a good cable release is a must.

Note: Many photographers acquire excellent cameras and lenses, yet skimp on adequate camera stands and cable releases. Sturdy tripods and copy stands are wise investments, and all cable releases are not the same. The most important function of a cable release is its ability to absorb the movement caused by your finger pressing the shutter release. Test cable releases by depressing their plungers (do not attach it to the camera while testing). A good cable release has a smooth action; a poor one offers resistance.

Self-Timer

The self-timer lever is the large lever on the right face (as you hold the camera) of the Pentax K2. It is capable of delaying the shutter from opening between 5 and 9 seconds. To cock the self-timer, pull the lever in an arc away from the lens. The amount of delay is dependent upon the arc the lever is moved. Swinging the lever all the way down until it stops yields the maximum 9-second delay.

The self-timer can be used in both Manual and Automatic modes. In the Automatic mode, light can enter the viewfinder through the eyepiece and affect the meter reading. Therefore, it is recommended that you cover the eyepiece when the meter reading is taken and the exposure is made. The K2 DMD has a viewfinder shutter blind incorporated in the body. The eyepiece on a camera model without this feature can easily be covered with a dark object.

The Pentax K2 self-timer can be interrupted after the timer has been activated. To do this, push the film advance lever in so it is flush with the camera; this will prevent the shutter from tripping. The timer will wind down, but the shutter will not release. You can then take a photo conventionally or reactivate the self-timer.

Depth-of-Field Preview

Depth of field refers to the area that is in apparent sharp focus in any photograph. Depth of field is determined by a combination of a lens' focal length and the selected aperture. Understanding depth of field allows the photographer to maximize or minimize the plane of sharpness in a photograph.

There are many charts, scales, and tables that you can use to compute depth of field, but observing it through the viewfinder is undoubtedly the best method. Normally, when you view the image through the viewfinder, the aperture is at its widest setting. Only when you trip the shutter does the iris close down to the set aperture. But the Pentax K2 has a depth-of-field preview feature that allows you to view the scene through the set aperture.

To check depth of field, set the lens to the f/stop you want to use to make the exposure. Then depress the depth-of-field preview button located on the right side of the camera, above the self-timer lever. Look through the viewfinder to preview the depth of field of the scene at that aperture. As the lens is stopped down, the view becomes darker and harder to see, but with patience and practice you will get the feel of it. When the button is released, full-aperture, bright viewing is restored.

Basic Flash Operation

The Pentax K2 has FP and X terminals on the side of the camera, near the rewind knob, and a separate X contact in the accessory hot shoe. Few photographers use FP, which was designed for a specific category of flash bulbs. Virtually all flash pictures nowadays are made with an electronic flash, which requires the X contact.

The K2 synchronizes with electronic flash at speeds up to and including 1/125 second. Regardless of how the flash is connected (with either a PC cord or hot shoe), the photographer must set the shutter speed dial manually to an appropriate shutter speed. If electronic flash is used at speeds faster than 1/125 second, only part of the frame will be exposed.

Asahi and other manufacturers have produced countless flash units that will function well with the K2, but each model offers different features. For best results, consult the flash unit's instruction book.

Pentax K2 DMD

Introduced in 1976, the K2 DMD was the final camera that Asahi added to the K family. The model designation "K2 DMD" is inscribed on the camera's face plate. DMD is the Asahi abbreviation for "Data, Motor Drive." Most of the functions and operations of the K2 DMD are identical to the K2, however the K2 DMD has some additional features: data back capability, a base plate that accepts a motor drive, an aperture readout port on the camera's face, an exposure lock function, a dual split-image/microprism focusing screen, and a built-in eyepiece cover.

The K2 DMD comes with a standard, non-data back version that is easily removable via a spring-loaded hinge pin. The optional data back replaces the conventional back, if desired. The data back is quite large by today's standards, and once installed, it must remain in place until the roll of film in the camera is completed or rewound. The data back is controlled by an "ON/OFF" switch located on the camera's base plate. The switch must be on for the data back to imprint data on the film.

The K2 DMD's base plate also contains the necessary couplings and contacts to attach the motor drive to the camera. The drive screws into the tripod socket, and the electrical connection is made through contact pins.

The small window in the center of the camera's face, just below the "NT" in PENTAX, allows the photographer to see the aperture setting while looking through the viewfinder.

The exposure lock function on the K2 DMD is automatically engaged when the mirror-lock lever is depressed and held. Pushing the mirror-lock lever up will lock the mirror and store the exposure reading for up to 10 minutes or until the shutter is tripped.

The standard K2 comes with either a split-image rangefinder or a microprism focusing screen; the K2 DMD's screen has both. The split-image rangefinder is the center portion of the viewfinder and the microprism surrounds it.

An eyepiece cover protects the viewfinder from receiving stray light. Although seldom used, this feature is a must for long exposures, self-timed photos, or any photo taken when the photographer's eye is not blocking the finder.

Pentax KM and KX

Because all the K-series cameras were introduced at about the same time, a sizable commotion was caused in the photographic industry—an industry that had grown accustomed to a gradual evolution of camera models. The KM and KX were introduced in 1975 and the K1000 was issued in 1976. On close inspection, these "new" cameras were actually updated Spotmatics in K-mount bodies. Here we'll discuss the similarities and differences between the KM and KX models. Another *Magic Lantern Guide* contains operating information on the K1000.

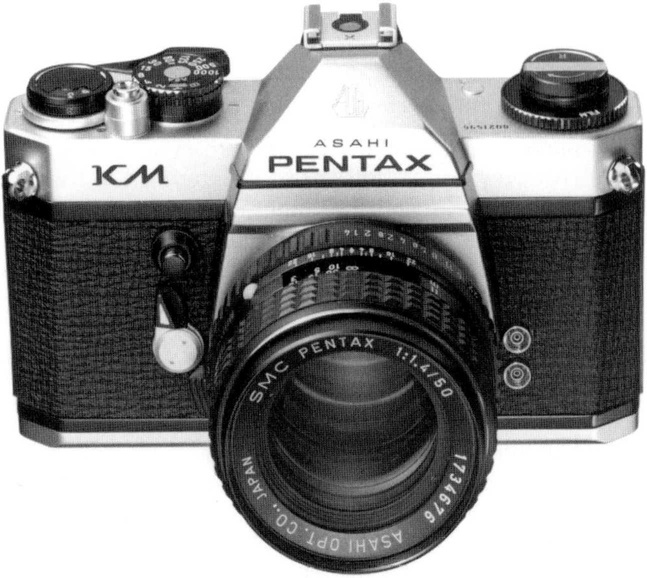

Asahi Pentax KM

Pentax KM and KX Specifications

Type:	35mm (24 x 36mm format), single-lens-reflex with built-in TTL light meter
Lens Mount:	Asahi Pentax K bayonet mount
Viewfinder:	Pentaprism; life-size view with 55mm lens; approximately 0.88x magnification with 50mm lens
Focusing Screen:	Split-image or microprism
Shutter:	Horizontally traveling, rubberized silk, focal plane shutter
Shutter Speeds:	1 second to 1/1000 second, plus B

Reflex Mirror:	Instant-return. Special shock absorbers reduce vibration.
Film Advance:	Rapid-wind lever. "Cocked" indicator adjacent to the shutter release button. 160° advance angle
Film Advance Stand-Off Angle:	KM = 10°; KX = 20°
Film Rewind:	Fold-out, rapid-rewind crank
Frame Counter:	Additive; automatic reset
Exposure Meter:	TTL, full-aperture metering. KM has a CdS meter that measures average brightness; center needle for correct exposure. KX has a Silicon-Photo-Diode meter for center-weighted metering; match needles in viewfinder for correct exposure.
Self-Timer:	Built-in self-timer on KM and KX has a variable delay of 5 to 13 seconds and an interrupt function.
Flash Synchronization:	
Electronic Flash Sync:	1/60 second by using the hot shoe or PC terminal on face of camera
FP Sync:	FP terminal on face of camera
Power Source:	
KM:	One 1.5v S76-type battery, or equivalent
KX:	Two 1.5v S76-type batteries, or equivalent
Dimensions with 50mm lens:	3.7 D x 3.6 H x 5.6″ W (94 x 91.4 x 143 mm), both models
Weight:	KM body: 21.8 oz. (622 g); with 50mm lens, 31 oz. (887 g). KX body: 22.1 oz. (631 g); with 50mm lens, 31.4 oz. (896 g).

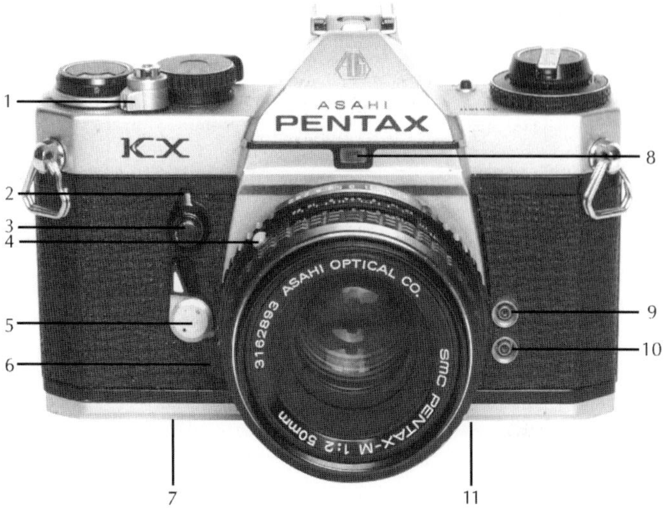

Asahi Pentax KX

The Pentax KX (pictured) is similar to the KM but with a few additional features.

1. **Shutter release lock (KX only)**
2. **Mirror lock-up lever (KX only)**
3. **Depth-of-field preview button**
4. **Lens mounting guide**
5. **Self-timer lever**
6. **Lens release lever**
7. **Rewind button (on base of camera)**
8. **Aperture readout window**
9. **FP flash sync terminal**
10. **X flash sync terminal**
11. **Battery chamber (on base of camera)**

Using the KM and KX

Battery Installation and Testing

The KM takes one S76 cell or the equivalent. The KX takes two S76 batteries, or the equivalent. The batteries in these two cameras power only their exposure meters. All other camera functions are performed mechanically. If your batteries die or you have none installed, only the exposure calculating function will fail; every other function will be operational.

To check the batteries on the KM, set the shutter speed dial to B and the ASA/ISO dial to 100. Observe the meter needle in the viewfinder; if the needle remains steady in the up position, the battery has adequate power.

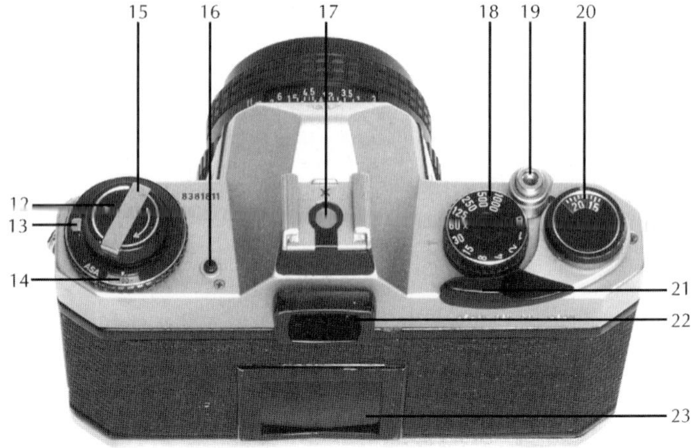

12. Rewind knob
13. ASA/ISO film speed release pin
14. ASA/ISO film speed window (KX only; KM has film reminder dial)
15. Rewind crank
16. Battery check button (KX only)
17. X sync accessory shoe
18. Shutter speed dial
19. Shutter release
20. Frame counter
21. Film advance lever
22. Viewfinder eyepiece
23. Memo holder (KX only)

To check batteries in the KX, depress the battery check button located on the top of the camera between the pentaprism and the rewind knob. If the black needle in the viewfinder drops to 125 or lower, the batteries contain adequate power.

Hint: All batteries have a limited shelf life, and batteries for these cameras are inexpensive. Pick a date that is easily remembered, like your birthday, and replace the camera batteries once a year. Regardless of how fresh your batteries are, always carry some spares.

Setting the Film Speed

The ISO dial can be set at any speed you desire. Usually the film manufacturers' recommendations should be observed, but at times, depending on the conditions, other settings may prove better. Some photographers use the film speed dial as if it were an exposure compensation device; for example, if they wish to "push" film speeds by rating the film higher and compensating in development, or "pull" film by shooting the film at a lower speed and adjusting the development. For those who wish to intentionally over- or underexpose film at a constant rate during a series of exposures, altering the film speed setting is a simple way to do so.

To set the film speed on the KM, lift the outer ring of the shutter speed dial and rotate it until the desired ISO setting appears in the film speed window and aligns with the orange index.

To set the film speed on the KX, depress the film speed release pin adjacent to the rewind knob and turn the outer ring of the film speed dial until the desired ISO setting is opposite the index mark by the ASA/ISO window.

Film Reminder Dial (KM)

The KM has a film reminder dial located on the ring that surrounds the rewind knob; the KX does not. The film reminder dial allows the photographer to set (in two separate windows) film type (black and white, daylight color, or tungsten color) and the number of exposures (the only choices are 20 or 36). This dial has no connection to any internal camera setting or function, it does only what its name suggests—it serves as a reminder.

Memo Holder (KX)

Though the KX does not have a film reminder dial, it does have a memo holder. It is located on the camera back, sized perfectly to fit a film box end or a handwritten note. Use it to remind yourself of the film type and number of exposures loaded.

Focusing Screens

Both of these cameras were originally equipped with either a microprism or a split-image focusing screen. See page 31 for more information on focusing.

Shutter Speed Dial

The shutter speed dial can be rotated in either direction, and the shutter speed can be selected before or after the shutter is cocked. When the shutter is cocked, the "cocked" indicator, located between the film advance lever and the shutter release button, turns red.

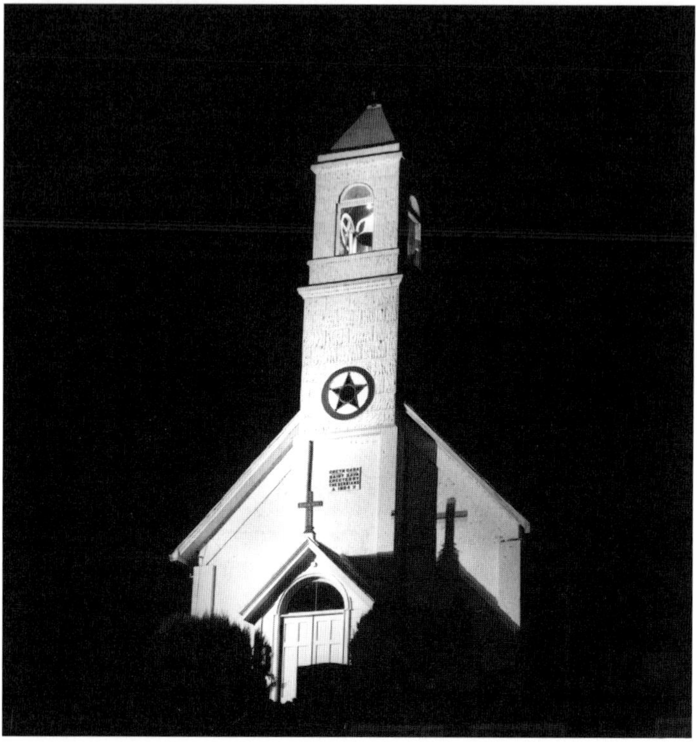

To take a photo with this much clarity at night, you have to use a tripod. A locking cable release also reduces the chance of camera shake.

The X at 1/60 second indicates the fastest electronic flash sync speed. The B (bulb) setting causes the shutter to stay open as long as the shutter release button is depressed. To reduce the chance of camera shake, use a tripod and a cable release that has a locking device when shooting in B.

Shutter Release Lock (KX)

The Pentax KX is equipped with a shutter release lock lever, an eccentric device that encircles the shutter release button. In its normal position, the shutter can be tripped. If flipped to its alternate position (an L will become visible on the top of the camera), it prevents the shutter release from being depressed. In the locked position, the shutter lock lever also switches the exposure meter off.

The shutter lock lever can also be used to lock the shutter open. If the shutter speed dial is set to B, the shutter release button is depressed, and the shutter lock lever switched to L, the shutter will remain open until the shutter lock lever is returned to its unlocked position. Long time exposures can be made this way, but a locking-type cable release will probably produce less camera vibration. Again, a tripod is recommended for shots such as these.

Light Meter Activation

On the KM the light meter is activated as soon as the lens cap is removed. Many photographers were concerned that a camera without an on/off switch would rapidly drain batteries; however we have found that batteries last as long in the KM as do batteries in cameras that contain on/off switches.

The light meter is activated on the KX when the film advance lever is in the stand-off position and the shutter release button is depressed halfway. To turn the light meter off, return the film advance lever to its flush position.

KX Viewfinder Exposure Data

Like the Spotmatic cameras, the KM shows only a "+," "–," and a needle to indicate overexposure, underexposure, or correct exposure (see page 56 for illustration).

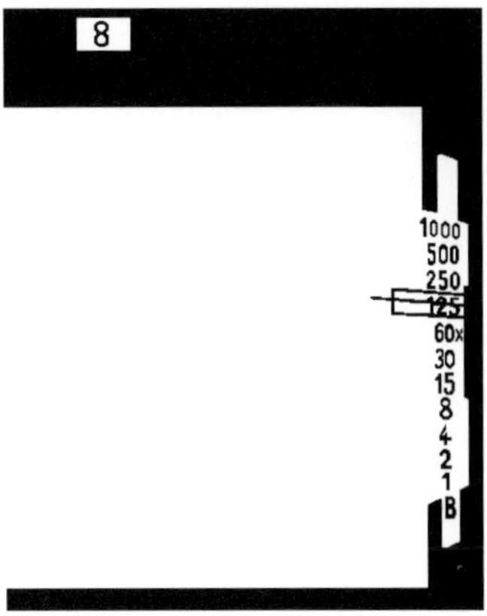

The KX's viewfinder is similar to that of the K2, but with an aperture readout at the top of the screen. Note also that the KX lacks the "Auto" setting and only has shutter speeds from 1 to 1/1000 second. Here, the shutter speed is set to the meter's recommendation of 1/125 second.

The KX contains a full-information viewfinder, in which both the set aperture and shutter speed are visible. The selected aperture is displayed in the small window at the top center of the finder, and shutter speeds are displayed along the right edge of the focusing screen. Notice that as you rotate the shutter speed dial, the blue-green needle indicates the selected speed. The black needle will overlap with the blue-green one when your exposure settings match the meter's suggested reading.

Setting Exposure

The key to setting exposure is to select the desired shutter speed first and then the aperture. We recommend doing it in this order because shutter speeds can not be interpolated, but the aperture can be set to intermediate positions. As a guide, choose a shutter speed that will be fast enough to prevent recording camera or subject movement. However, don't squander exposure control on needlessly high shutter speeds, since an overly fast shutter speed will reduce the range of apertures available to you.

On the KM, select the shutter speed, then turn the aperture ring until the light meter needle (located on the right side of the viewfinder) is centered in the horizontal channel. The viewfinder display on this camera is identical to that of the Spotmatic (see page 56). At the top of the metering indicator is a "+," at the bottom, "–." If you wish to deviate from the metered exposure, for instance in backlit or complex lighting situations, adjust the shutter speed or aperture until the needle points in the direction of overexposure (+) or underexposure (–), as desired.

To follow the meter's recommended exposure with the KX, activate the light meter, and then adjust the exposure until the black and blue-green needles align in the viewfinder.

Multiple Exposures

Multiple exposures are easy to accomplish with the KM and KX. Make the first exposure in the usual way, then remove any slack in the film by turning the rewind knob. While holding the tension in the rewind knob (or crank), depress the film rewind button, then move the film advance lever through its normal 160° arc. This cocks the shutter without advancing the film. Now the shutter can be tripped, causing a double exposure. This cycle can be repeated to create any number of overlapping exposures. When the final exposure has been

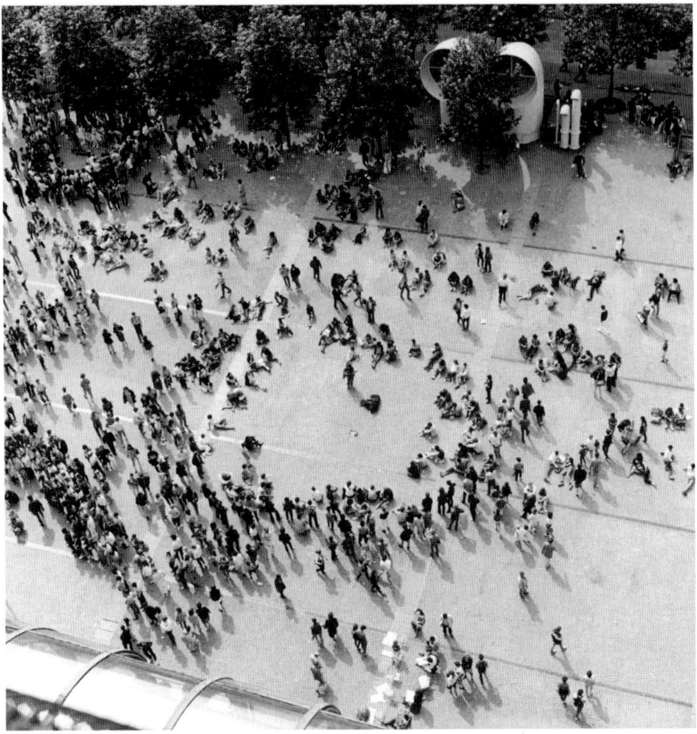

Some shots require less concentration on the technical aspects and more concentration on the compositional aspects of the scene. In a situation such as this, depth of field was unimportant, as the people were all approximately the same distance away from the camera. The choice of shutter speed was also not crucial since there was no rapid movement.

completed on the frame, make one blank exposure to avoid overlapping the next image onto the multiple exposure frame, as registration may not be exact. Remember, when making multiple exposures, some exposure compensation is usually required, unless you are shooting a subject against a black background.

Mirror Lock-up Lever (KX)

The Pentax KX contains a mirror lock-up feature; the KM does not. The KX's mirror lock-up lever is located on the face of the camera, just above the self-timer lever.

During normal picture-taking operation, when the shutter is tripped, the reflex mirror swings up to allow light to strike the film. After the exposure has been made, the mirror drops to allow light to be reflected into the viewfinder again. Mirror movement causes a small amount of vibration; not enough to degrade normal pictures, but enough to affect high-magnification photography, especially when using long telephoto lenses, telescopes, or microscopes.

Before using the mirror lock-up lever, focus, compose, and make the exposure settings. Make sure that the camera is mounted to a tripod, copy stand, or some other device that will keep it from moving once composition has been achieved. To engage the mirror-lock mechanism, swing the mirror lock-up lever in a clockwise direction (away from the lens) as far as it will travel. While holding the lever, depress the button located inside the lever's hub. (When used alone, this is the depth-of-field preview button.)

Once locked up, the mirror will stay up until it is released. To release, return the mirror-locking lever to its original position. The mirror can be locked or returned to its normal position before or after the shutter is cocked.

Self-Timer

The KM and KX cameras contain a built-in self-timer. Self-timers are available as optional accessories at most good camera stores. The accessory self-timer screws into the shutter release button, just as a cable release does.

The self-timer lever is the large silver-colored lever located on the right side of the camera face, just below the model designation. To take a self-timed photo, first cock the shutter. Then cock the self-timer by rotating it clockwise (away from the lens). The 5- to 13-second delay time is controlled by the distance the lever is rotated; 90° yields approximately a 5-second delay, rotating it all the way until it stops yields the maximum delay time of 13 seconds. Cocking the self-timer lever exposes a smaller lever that is concealed when the master lever is in its "up" position. The self-timer sequence is started by moving the small lever, but remember, the shutter must first be cocked.

If you change your mind after the self-timer has been activated, you can stop it by rotating the start lever back to its original position.

Note: The interrupt function will work only if done before the self-timer lever has reached the 90° position.

Do not leave the self-timer lever in its interrupted position for an extended time; it will eventually weaken the spring. If you cannot do it sooner, cycle the self-timer mechanism when the roll of film has been completed.

Depth-of-Field Preview

Depth of field is the term used to describe the area in a picture that is in sharp focus. There are several ways to determine depth of field. Most single focal length lenses contain a depth-of-field scale; some cameras are equipped with a depth-of-field preview mechanism.

The Pentax KM and KX both have a depth-of-field preview button. The depth-of-field preview button is located just above the self-timer lever. On the KX, the mirror lock-up lever surrounds it.

Observing depth of field through the viewfinder requires patience and skill. Many photographers prefer to use the scale found on select lenses, the depth-of-field charts found in many publications, or better yet, the depth-of-field dial contained in the *KODAK Pocket Photoguide*. This guide presents a simple way to compute depth of field for any focal length lens, including zooms. Most camera stores stock this small, handy, inexpensive guide, which contains many additional bits of useful information.

To preview the depth of field, depress the depth-of-field preview button. It is engaged only as long as it is depressed; when released, it returns the aperture to its widest setting for bright, full-aperture viewing. To preview depth of field, rotate the aperture ring while depressing the preview button, and observe the image through the viewfinder. The image will be darker than usual, and judging depth of field in this way will take some getting used to. Repeated practice is the best way to learn how to use the depth-of-field preview function.

Basic Flash Operation

The Pentax KM and KX have an X contact on the hot shoe and a PC terminal for X synchronization on the camera's face. In addition, they have a second PC terminal marked "FP." X terminals are for electronic flash synchronization; FP is for synchronization with flash bulbs. Few photographers use flash bulbs today, but flash bulb users or those who are curious can find more information in the *Flash Photography* chapter.

If an electronic flash with a hot shoe is mounted in the camera's flash shoe, proper electrical contact is automatically established. But, if contact is made with a connecting cord, care must be taken to correctly insert the cord into the PC terminal marked "X."

With electronic flash, both cameras must be set at shutter speeds of 1/60 second or slower. Electronic flash at shutter speeds of 1/125 second or faster will result in proper exposure only on part of the frame; the rest of the frame will be dark or possibly blank.

Both cameras can be used with manual or automatic flash units. They can be used with Pentax flash units and aftermarket flash units. The number of flash units that function with K-series cameras is countless. For accurate compatibility and operational data, consult the flash unit's instruction book, seek help in a friendly camera store, or as a last resort, experiment on unimportant shots.

Caution: *The K-series cameras do not have dedicated flash functions, therefore, sophisticated flash units must be used in a mode that is compatible with the cameras, such as A or M.*

Pentax M Series

Camera and lens size are not important considerations to every photographer, but many prefer a compact, lightweight outfit over a heavy, bulky one. This is one of the main reasons why Asahi redesigned their camera line with the M series. In 1973 Olympus took the camera market by storm with their tiny OM-1. In 1977 Pentax cameras became part of this small camera trend with the introduction of the ME and MX compact SLR cameras.

The cameras in the Pentax M series have more things in common than first meet the eye. To prove the point, we will first study the Pentax ME, ME Super, and the MX, comparing and contrasting features and functions. These cameras will help you understand the MEF's operation. The MG, MV, and MV-1 are also covered in this chapter. Introduced between the years 1977 and 1982, the M series gradually made a bold transition into the electronic era.

This transition included a subtle name change. When the name Asahi was placed on a model, the typeface was initially made much smaller than it once was, and the name Pentax became the prominent identifier. Eventually, most cameras in this series would bear only the Pentax name, without the Asahi inscription.

Less subtle was the evolution to electronic shutters. At that time, the entire camera manufacturing industry was headed in this direction. Some camera companies were ahead of Asahi, some followed slowly behind. Electronic shutters made possible stepless shutter speeds and more shutter speed accuracy than had been possible with mechanically timed shutters.

One camera in this series, the MEF, placed Asahi in the autofocus SLR arena. Most of the major Japanese camera manufacturers were cautiously entering this new era with tentative steps. However, Asahi was one of many manufacturers that made revolutionary autofocus changes.

To fully explain the operating systems of this camera family, we will start with the major specifications of the most significant and most popular cameras of the series.

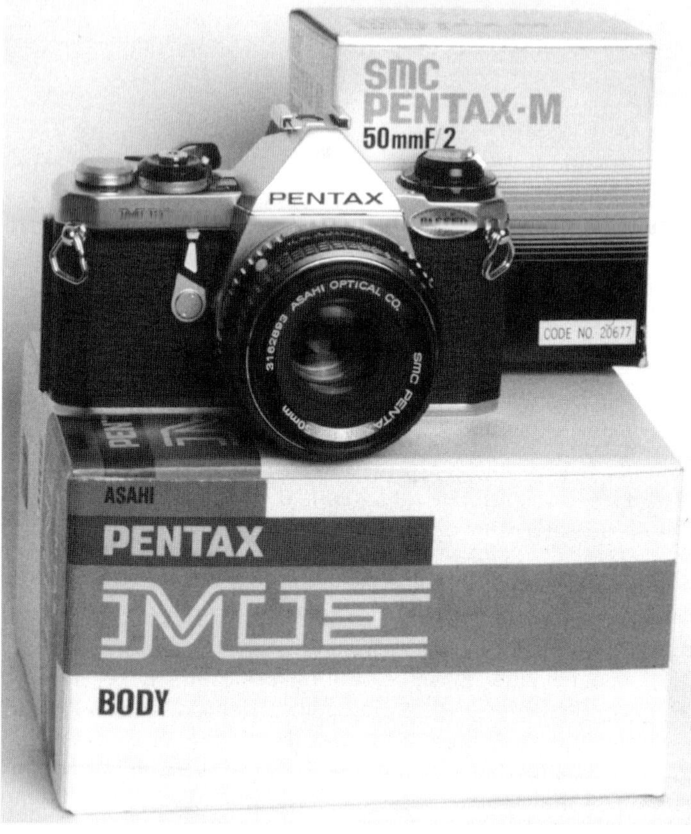

Asahi Pentax ME

Pentax ME, ME Super, and MX Specifications

Introduced:
- **ME and MX:** 1977
- **ME Super:** 1980

Type: 35mm (24 x 36mm format), single-lens-reflex

Lens Mount: Asahi Pentax K bayonet mount

Shutter:	
ME and ME Super:	Seiko MFC vertically traveling, metal focal plane shutter
MX:	Horizontally traveling, rubberized silk focal plane shutter
Shutter Speeds:	
ME:	Automatic shutter speeds, electronically controlled between 8 seconds and 1/1000 second. Manual mechanical speed of 1/100 second, plus B
ME Super:	Automatic shutter speeds electronically controlled (stepless) between 4 seconds and 1/2000 second. Manual mechanical settings of 1/125 second, plus B
MX:	Mechanically controlled speeds from 1 second to 1/1000 second, plus B
Focusing Screen:	Factory-equipped with a split image/microprism focusing screen. MX has 9 interchangeable screens.
Film Advance:	
ME and ME Super:	Single-stroke, rapid-wind lever with 135° throw and 30° stand-off angle
MX:	Ratchet-type rapid-wind lever with 162° throw and a stand-off angle of 20°
Film Rewind:	Rewind knob with fold-out rapid-rewind crank
Frame Counter:	Additive, automatic reset
Film Loading:	"Magic-needle, quick/sure" loading
Film Chamber Door:	Detachable; interchangeable with accessory backs
Exposure Meter:	Open-aperture, center-weighted TTL metering with Gallium-Photo-Diode (GPD) cells
Exposure Compensation:	1/4x to 4x (–2 to +2 stops) on ME and ME Super
Self-Timer:	
ME and ME Super:	Shutter release is delayed 4 to 12 seconds by cocking and pushing up on the self-timer lever.
MX:	Shutter release is delayed 4 to 12 seconds

	by cocking the self-timer lever and pressing the self-timer start button.
Viewfinder:	Pentaprism finder; ME and ME Super, 92% viewing. MX, 95% viewing
Flash Synchronization:	
ME:	1/100 second
ME Super:	1/125 second
MX:	1/60 second
Power Source:	Two 1.5v S76-type batteries, or equivalent
Dimensions (body only):	
ME:	2 D x 3.3 H x 5.2″W (49.5 x 82.5 x 131 mm)
ME Super:	2 D x 3.3 H x 5.3″W (49.5 x 83 x 131.5 mm)
MX:	2 D x 3.3 H x 5.4″W (49.5 x 82.5 x 135.5 mm)
Weight (body only):	
ME:	16.1 oz. (460 g)
ME Super:	15.8 oz. (445 g)
MX:	17.3 oz. (495 g)

Using the Pentax M Cameras

All Pentax M-series cameras operate in much the same manner; differences are found only in the way that exposure is controlled. What follows is a discussion of the control and operation of the three primary M cameras, the ME, ME Super, and MX. Later we will discuss the other models in the M family, and their slight, but sometimes not so insignificant, differences.

Battery Installation and Testing

The Pentax M-series cameras require two 1.5v S76 batteries or equivalent. Whenever possible use silver-oxide batteries; they outlast any other type and perform better than their lower-priced counterparts.

To check the batteries' power, depress the shutter release button halfway while looking through the viewfinder. If the LED illuminates, the batteries are good. If the LED flickers, the batteries are weak. If there is no LED illumination, the batteries are completely exhausted. Take any battery-failure warning seriously and replace the failing batteries as soon as possible. And always carry spares in your camera bag.

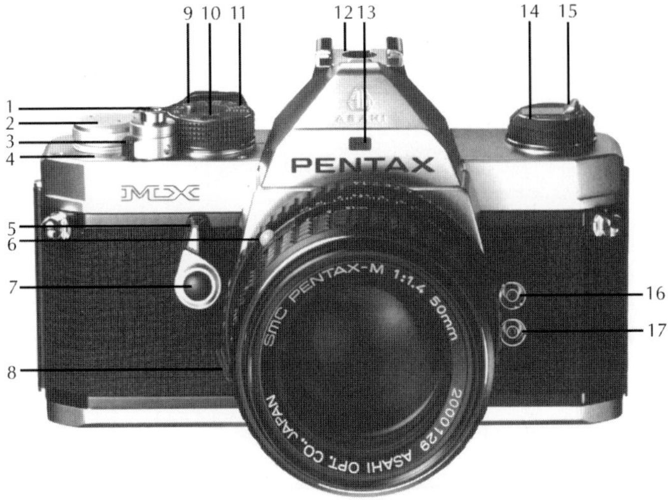

Asahi Pentax MX

1. **Shutter release button**
2. **Rapid-wind film advance lever**
3. **Shutter release lock**
4. **Frame counter**
5. **Self-timer lever**
6. **Lens mounting index**
7. **Self-timer start button**
8. **Lens release lever**
9. **ASA/ISO film speed dial release button**
10. **ASA/ISO film speed window**
11. **Shutter speed dial**
12. **X sync accessory shoe**
13. **Aperture readout window**
14. **Rewind knob/Back cover release**
15. **Film rewind crank**
16. **X flash sync terminal**
17. **FP flash sync terminal**

Batteries will operate all ME and MX model cameras approximately 10,000 times, but they may not have a shelf life of much longer than one year. Treat your camera to fresh batteries every time you have a birthday or on any other easily remembered annual event.

Hint: Store the camera in the "L" or locked position to prevent accidental battery drain.

Loading Film

It is advisable to set the shutter speed to a manually controlled

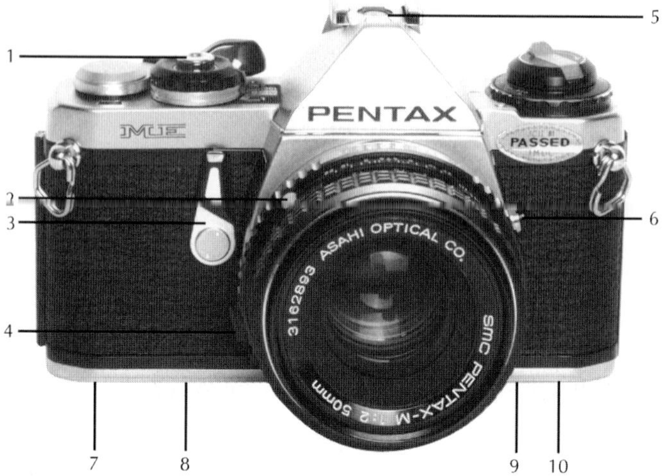

Asahi Pentax ME
The Asahi Pentax ME (pictured) and ME Super are very similar, with only a few variations.

1. **Shutter release button**
2. **Lens alignment dot**
3. **Self-timer**
4. **Lens release lever**
5. **Accessory hot shoe**
6. **X flash sync terminal**
7. **Film transport coupler (on base of camera, ME Super, MV-1 only)**
8. **Film rewind button (on base of camera)**
9. **Battery chamber (on base of camera)**
10. **Power winder point (on base of camera, ME, MV-1 only)**

shutter speed (*not* Automatic mode) before loading any M-series Pentax camera (e.g., ME, ME Super, MEF, MG, MV, MV-1). Loading a camera with the shutter in the "AUTO" position while the lens cap is on or while loading in a dark place can cause such long delays that the unsuspecting photographer may fear the camera has jammed. Select the speed that is marked as the X sync speed.

With the introduction of the M-series cameras, Pentax redesigned their film take-up spools. Instead of having slots in the spool, the new spools were surrounded by white plastic pins called "magic needles." The film leader can be inserted between any of these white pins, making film loading easy.

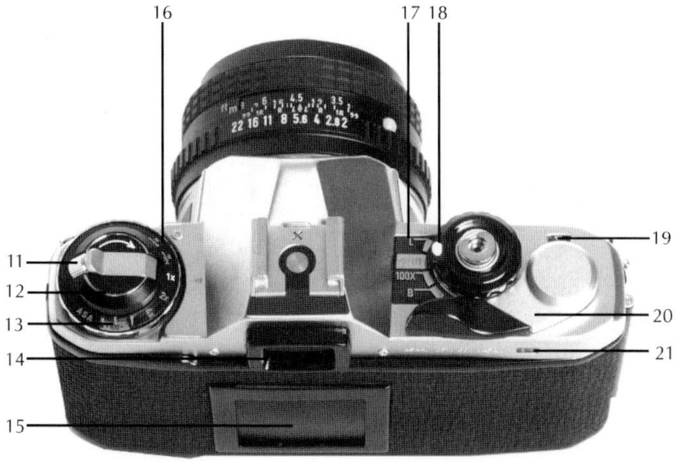

11. Film rewind crank
12. Rewind knob/Back cover release
13. ASA/ISO film speed indicator
14. Eyepiece
15. Memo holder
16. Exposure compensation dial
17. Exposure mode/Shutter speed control panel (ME Super allows manual shutter speed selection)
18. Exposure mode index button
19. Frame counter
20. Film advance lever
21. Film advance and rewind indicator

Film Advance and Rewind Indicator

The Pentax ME and ME Super have a film advance and rewind indicator that verifies that the film is traveling either forward onto the take-up spool or back into the cassette. The indicator is located on the right side of the camera back, just below the film advance lever. The window contains vertical stripes that move any time the film is traveling. Observe the indicator when advancing a new roll of film to the first exposure and when rewinding the film. Using this guide can prevent embarrassing film loading or unloading mistakes.

Advancing Film

The film advance lever stores in a position that is virtually flush with the camera top. The lever has a stand-off position to facilitate rapid film advancement, even when the photographer is not looking at the camera. The advance lever can be placed in either the cocked or "at-rest" position at any time.

To advance the film one frame, wind the film advance lever through its complete arc. The Pentax MX allows film to also be advanced with a ratchet motion, although most photographers prefer a smoother, single-stroke advance. The ME and ME Super have the single-stroke advance.

If film advancement feels rough, stiff, or unusual, stop! Forcing the advance lever may rip the film or pull its end out of the cassette. At one time or another, everyone has forgotten how many exposures have been taken or what length the roll was to begin with. At the first warning that film advancement is not going smoothly, discover why. Most scenarios of this type are easily solved by rewinding the film and loading a new roll.

Setting the Film Speed

To set the film speed (on all cameras except the MX), lift up the ASA/ISO dial surrounding the film rewind knob, and turn it until the desired film speed appears in the window opposite the film speed index.

The Pentax MX has an ASA/ISO dial lock release button; it is the shiny button next to the 15 on the shutter speed dial. To select a film speed, depress the ASA/ISO dial lock release and turn the rim of the shutter speed dial until the desired film speed is in the window and aligned with the index.

Memo Holder

Most cameras of this era contain a memo holder. The memo holder is located on the back of the camera, conveniently sized to hold a film box end (which states the film type and number of exposures) or a handwritten note. For photographers who change film types often or who do not finish a roll at the end of each shooting session, the memo holder can be a valuable reminder.

MX Interchangeable Focusing Screens

The Pentax MX affords the photographer the ability to interchange focusing screens (the ME and ME Super do not). At the time of the camera's manufacture, eight accessory screens were available, plus the split-image/microprism SC-1 focusing screen that was

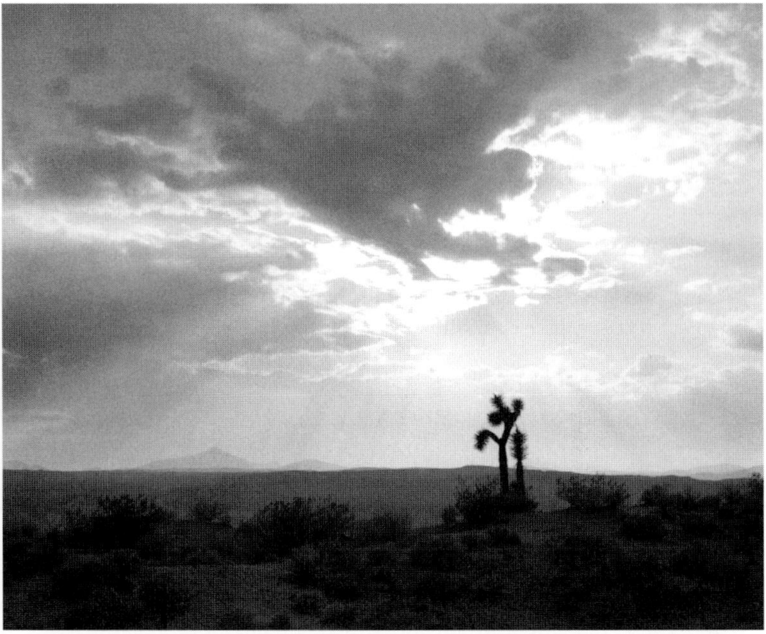

The Pentax MX offers the photographer the option of nine focusing screens, each with its own specialized application. The SG screen is ideal for photographing architecture or landscapes with strong horizon lines. Its horizontal and vertical grid lines help ensure proper compositional alignment and subject placement.

supplied in the camera at the time of purchase. See pages 176 and 177 for more information.

To remove the standard screen, use the tweezers supplied with the interchangeable screen. Focusing screens are easily damaged; never touch one with your bare fingers and never attempt to wipe or polish one.

Focusing screens are interchanged in the area above the mirror, in the mirror box. With no lens mounted on the camera, the focusing screen is visible in the top of the mirror box. To remove the screen, use the end of the tweezers to pull the screen-retaining pin toward the lens mount opening. This action causes the focusing screen to flip down. Remove the screen by grasping the screen's handling tab delicately with the tweezers.

To install a screen, reverse this procedure. Place the screen on the screen frame, push it back to its original position, and make sure it is locked into place.

Screens should be changed only in a clean environment. Seek a dust-free location and avoid any air currents—once a foreign object lands on a focusing screen it is difficult to remove. The only possible screen cleaning tools available to a photographer are those that blow a screen clean, such as canned air or a puff blower.

Caution: *Never touch or wipe a focusing screen with even the softest brush, cloth, or tissue!*

Controlling Exposure

The Pentax ME was designed to be used as an automatic camera, the Pentax MX as a manually controlled camera, and the ME Super to be easily used in either mode.

Locking the Shutter

Both the Pentax ME and ME Super have a white button on the ring surrounding the shutter release button. This is the exposure mode index button, which serves as both the shutter speed indicator and lock. Setting it in the "L" position prevents the shutter from being released accidentally. To lock the shutter, depress the exposure mode index button and turn the exposure mode control dial to the "L" position.

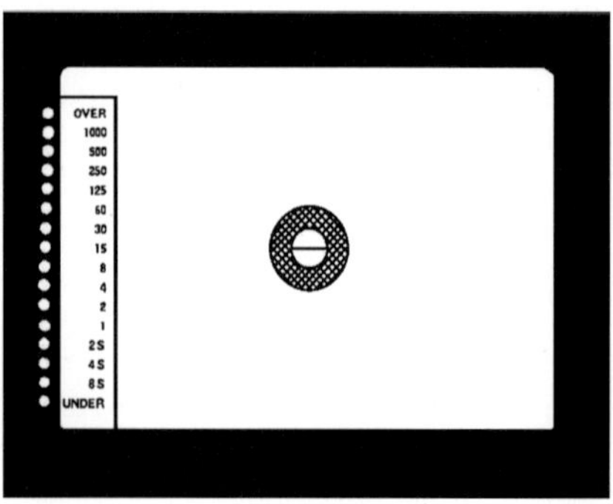

The viewfinder display on the ME includes a list of possible shutter speeds and under- and overexposure warnings. A red LED will light next to the currently set shutter speed as well as the appropriate exposure warning, if necessary.

ME Automatic Exposure Control

To set the camera to Automatic (Aperture-Priority) exposure mode, depress the exposure mode index button and rotate the exposure mode control dial (the ring surrounding the shutter release) until the button is adjacent to the word "AUTO." The electronic shutter of the Pentax ME works in Automatic mode at any shutter speed between 8 seconds and 1/1000 second. The shutter speed numbers are visible in the viewfinder. The LEDs on the left side of the viewfinder will alert you to over- and underexposure and will indicate the selected shutter speed.

To activate the LEDs and the exposure meter, depress the shutter release button halfway while the film advance lever is in its stand-off position. At this point, one of 16 LEDs will glow, indicating the shutter speed that has been automatically selected by the camera's metering system. If the automatically selected speed is not satisfactory (or if the "over" or "under" LED glows), turn the aperture ring until the system selects a more appropriate shutter speed. When both f/stop and shutter speed are satisfactory, depress the shutter release button fully to take the picture.

ME Super Automatic Exposure Control

In the Automatic mode, the Pentax ME Super functions in the same basic way as the Pentax ME, with some refinements and additional user-friendly features.

To activate the Pentax ME Super's autoexposure system, set the exposure mode control dial to "AUTO" (as described in the ME section, above), and depress the shutter release button slightly while looking into the viewfinder. The correct amount of pressure on the shutter release button will activate one LED along the side of the viewfinder screen.

***Caution**: Too much pressure will prematurely trip the shutter.*

Select the desired aperture and shutter speed combination as you would with the Pentax ME—rotating the lens' aperture ring causes the shutter speed to change accordingly.

There is no need to maintain finger pressure on the shutter release button; once activated, it will remain on for approximately 20 to 35 seconds. If it goes out before the exposure is taken, another slight press on the shutter release button will reactivate the meter.

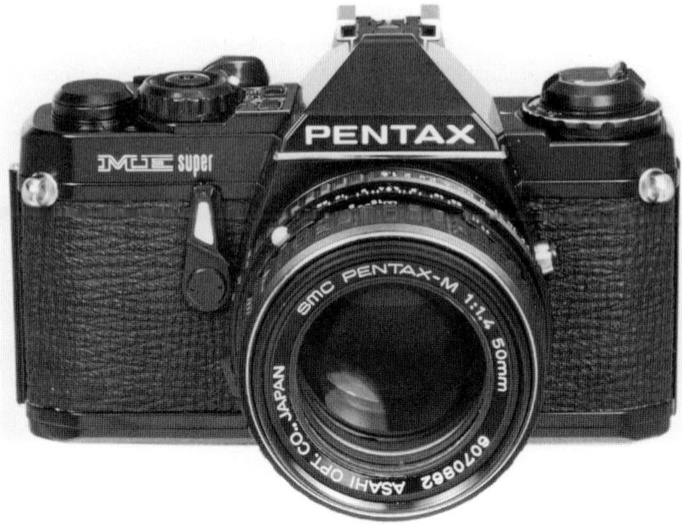

The Pentax ME Super offers a full range of shutter speeds from 4 seconds to 1/2000 second in Manual mode.

The Pentax ME Super automatically selects shutter speeds from 4 seconds to 1/2000 second in Auto mode. The viewfinder LEDs next to the shutter speeds ranging from 1/60 to 1/2000 second are green, as Pentax considers this the "safe zone" for hand-held shots. Shutter speeds of 1/30 second to 4 seconds are indicated by yellow LEDs, suggesting that some precautionary camera support is recommended.

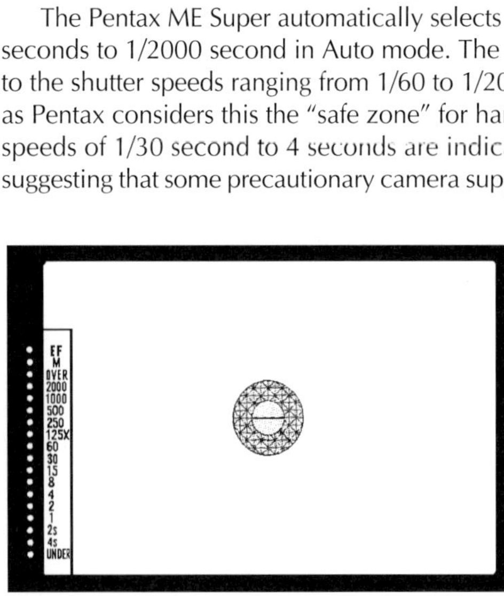

The ME Super's viewfinder display shows you the set shutter speed (from 4 seconds to 1/2000 second), warns of over- or underexposure, alerts you that you're in Manual exposure mode (M), and reminds you that exposure compensation has been set (EF).

A red LED will glow next to the word "OVER" or "UNDER" in the viewfinder if the exposure is beyond the metered, "correct" exposure range. If the "OVER" LED is illuminated, choosing a smaller aperture (higher f/number) will usually solve the problem. High-speed films and/or extremely bright light may, however, require that you use a light-reducing (neutral-density) filter.

The red LED adjacent to the word "UNDER" warns of underexposure. If this occurs, try opening the lens to its widest aperture (smallest f/number), or find a way to support the camera, set the shutter to "B" (bulb), and do a time exposure. Using a flash is also an option.

Caution: *The shutter will seem to jam on the ME or ME Super if the shutter release button is tripped while the camera is in the "AUTO" position and the lens is covered with a lens cap, or if the shutter is tripped while the camera is in an extremely dark place. If this occurs, turn the shutter speed dial to 100X or 125X and the shutter will close. After the shutter is released, remember to reset the dial to "AUTO" for Automatic mode.*

There are two additional LEDs in the viewfinder, "M" (Manual exposure mode) and "EF" (Exposure compensation Factor, reminding you that exposure compensation has been set). These are discussed on the following pages.

ME Super Manual Exposure Control

The Pentax ME Super has the following positions on its exposure mode control panel: "L" (Lock), "AUTO" (Automatic), "M" (Manual), "125X" (mechanically operated shutter speed that synchronizes with electronic flash), and "B" (bulb).

To use the ME Super in Manual mode, set the exposure mode control dial to "M." Then, depress the shutter release button lightly while looking through the viewfinder. Once the LED display is illuminated, there is no need to keep pressure on the button; one touch keeps it lit for about 20 to 35 seconds, or until the shutter is tripped. If the display goes dark and additional metering time is needed, partially depress the shutter release button to reactivate the meter.

When the Pentax ME Super is set in Manual mode, the "M" LED illuminates in the viewfinder display. This reminder is credited with saving many shots—often after a shooting session photographers assume that their camera will magically go back to the Automatic mode. The "M" illuminated in the viewfinder display reminds them that the camera is still in Manual mode.

Setting exposure in Manual mode is simple. The photographer may obtain the proper setting by selecting either shutter speed or aperture. Apertures are set on the lens aperture ring. There is no aperture readout in the viewfinder display. Shutter speeds are selected using the push buttons adjacent to the exposure mode control dial. With the meter active, pressing the forward button increases the shutter speed, the other decreases the shutter speed. Both cycle through the shutter speeds continuously; once the top button reaches the fastest speed, it proceeds to the slowest and again moves up the scale, and once the bottom button reaches the slowest speed, it moves on to the fastest, proceeding down the scale. Release the button when the desired shutter speed's LED is illuminated in the viewfinder display.

The shutter speed increase button is located adjacent to the shutter lock symbol ("L") on the exposure mode control panel. The shutter speed decrease button is located adjacent to the "125X."

If the system is activated and the manually selected exposure does not match the meter's recommended exposure, the "M" LED, an LED indicating the selected shutter speed, and either the "OVER" or "UNDER" LED will be illuminated. Usually, turning the aperture ring or pressing a shutter speed control button will cause the "OVER" or "UNDER" LED to be extinguished. When the shutter speed LED and the "M" LED are the only ones illuminated in the viewfinder display, the set exposure matches the meter's suggested reading.

If no amount of exposure adjustment turns off the "OVER" LED, a light-reducing (neutral-density) filter, slower film, or some method of light reduction is required. If the "UNDER" LED cannot be eliminated, even if the lens is wide open and the shutter is at its slowest speed, try a faster lens, faster (higher) speed film, introducing more light (flash or hot lights), or a time exposure.

Mechanical Shutter Speeds

The Pentax ME and ME Super have shutters that are electronically timed. If the batteries fail, these cameras can function at only two shutter speeds. The ME can function at 1/100 second and B, the ME Super at 1/125 second and B. The cameras also synchronize with electronic flash at these shutter speeds (100X or 125X, respectively). "X" is the symbol for electronic flash; whenever it is seen on a camera, it implies electronic flash synchronization.

"B" is the symbol for "bulb." It has been used since the days when shutters were tripped with pneumatic bulbs connected to the shutter through an air hose. In recent years, B has come to mean time exposures. If time exposures were battery-dependent, batteries would be quickly exhausted. Fortunately B is a mechanical setting, so no battery drain occurs. When the camera is placed on a tripod and the shutter is tripped using a cable release and held open for prolonged times, no battery drain occurs.

MX Shutter Speed Dial

The shutter speed dial on the Pentax MX can be turned in either direction, before or after the shutter has been cocked (the shutter is cocked when the film has been wound to a new frame). The "shutter-cocked" indicator turns red when the shutter is cocked, and it turns black after the shutter has been tripped. This indicator is adjacent to the shutter release button and the shutter speed dial.

The numbers on the shutter speed dial represent fractions of a second. The "B" (bulb) setting will keep the shutter open as long as the shutter release button is depressed. The shutter release lock lever surrounding the shutter release can be used to prevent accidental exposures, because it will not allow the shutter to be released, even when the shutter is cocked. It can also be used to lock the shutter open for long time exposures.

To take long time exposures using the shutter release lock, first set the shutter speed dial to B, press the shutter release, and rotate the shutter release lock to its locked position. The shutter will remain open until the locking lever is turned to its unlocked position. Long time exposures are usually made with the camera perfectly still, otherwise the image will be blurred. A sturdy tripod and locking-type cable release are highly recommended. (A locking-type cable release will not transfer any movement to the camera, whereas the shutter release locking button may.)

The X, located at the 1/60 second position, represents the fastest shutter speed that will synchronize with electronic flash.

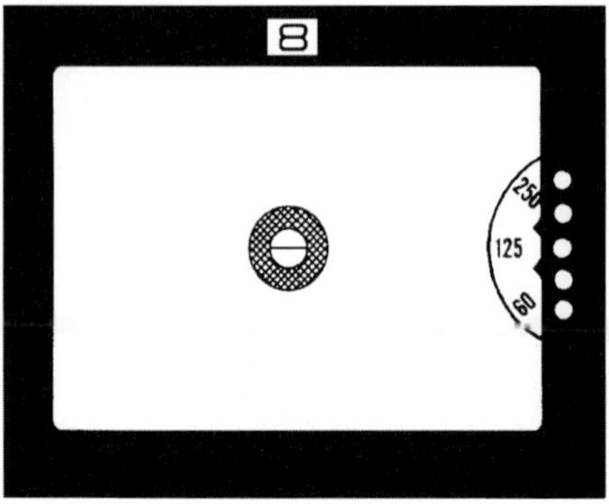

The MX viewfinder display has an aperture readout and a shutter speed scale that displays only three speeds at a time. The center shutter speed, falling between the two pointers, is the one currently set. The LEDs at right are color-coded to indicate exposure accuracy.

MX Exposure Control

The Pentax MX has a full-information viewfinder: f/stop, shutter speed, and over- and underexposure data are all visible. Unlike the ME and ME Super, the selected aperture can be seen at the top. Three shutter speeds are visible on the right side of the focusing screen; the one in the center corresponds to the speed selected on the shutter speed dial.

The exposure meter on the MX is activated when the film advance lever is in its 20° stand-off position and the shutter release button is depressed halfway. At this point, one of five LEDs on the right side of the viewfinder is illuminated. Turn either the aperture ring or the shutter speed dial to set the desired exposure and read the exposure information LEDs on the right side of the finder. The exposure is correct when the green (center) LED is glowing. There are two LEDs on either side of the green one. If the upper orange LED is illuminated, 1/2-stop overexposure is indicated; if the lower orange LED is lit, 1/2-stop underexposure is indicated. If either of the two red LEDs is lit, the exposure is off by at least one full stop.

Exposure Compensation

Exposure compensation is used in conjunction with a camera's Automatic exposure mode. It is not needed when a camera's exposure is being set manually. The Pentax ME and ME Super feature an exposure compensation dial, however the MX does not. The exposure compensation dial encircles the film rewind knob; its index is located on the camera body's top plate. To engage the compensation feature, simply turn the dial until the amount of

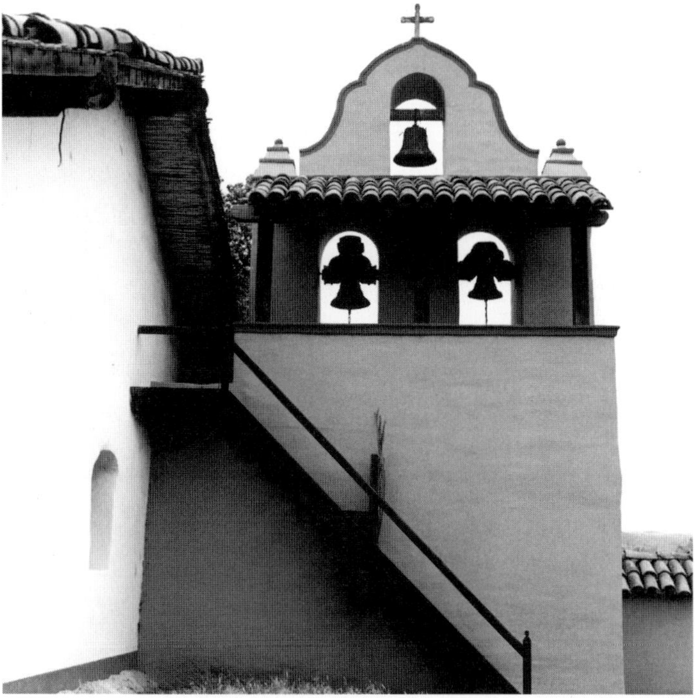

This photo is composed of stark shapes and forms. Careful exposure meter readings are necessary to control a backlit shot like this. Using an 18% gray card will render the tones accurately on a gray scale, however further exposure adjustment may be necessary to produce dramatic effect.

compensation is set opposite the index. No compensation, or 1x, is the normal setting, full numbers increase exposure, and fractional numbers decrease exposure in a range of 4x to 1/4x. For example, 2x yields twice the exposure recommended by the light meter, while 1/2x cuts the exposure in half. In the ME Super's viewfinder, the LED will light next to the letters "EF" to remind you that an exposure compensation factor has been set and that you may want to reset it before you take the next exposure.

Exposure compensation sounds simple, but it takes practice and experience to accurately determine how much compensation is needed. Advanced or alternate metering techniques, such as

Manual exposure, 18% gray card readings, and exposure bracketing, are often used by photographers when they suspect that an automatic setting will not produce the desired result.

Multiple Exposures

To make multiple exposures, expose the first image in the conventional way. Next, make sure there is no film slack in the cassette. (This is done by turning the rewind lever until tension is felt.) After the slack has been eliminated, hold the rewind lever, depress the rewind button, and cock the shutter by winding the film advance lever once. (This procedure recocks the shutter without advancing the film.) The second exposure is now ready to be recorded. Additional exposures can be made on the frame by repeating this same procedure. Exposure compensation may be necessary depending on the subject, background, and number of exposures being made.

When the last multiple exposure has been made, make one blank exposure. Most camera film advance registration systems are not precise enough to guarantee that there will not be a slight image overlap, so take a blank frame for safety.

Self-Timer

The self-timer lever is the large lever located on the face of the Pentax M-series cameras. It is capable of delaying the shutter opening (each camera varies, but most have a range of approximately 4 seconds to 15 seconds). To cock the self-timer lever, swing it in an arc away from the lens. The amount of delay is dependent upon the distance that the lever has been moved. Naturally, swinging the lever all the way to its stopping point will yield its maximum delay time.

Self-timers will function in either the Manual or Automatic mode. When the self-timer is activated and the camera is in the Automatic mode, light may enter the viewfinder through the eyepiece. To prevent stray light from causing an erroneous automatic exposure setting, cover the eyepiece with an eyepiece cap. If one is not available, any dark, hand-crafted cover will probably work.

Most cameras in the M series (ME, ME Super, MG) have self-timers that are activated by a slight upward push on the self-timer lever. The Pentax MX has a self-timer release button that is not visible until the self-timer lever is cocked. Depressing this button starts the delay sequence.

To learn how a self-timer really works, experiment with it while the camera is empty. Test its minimum and maximum delay times to determine your camera's exact behavior. It is advisable to exercise the self-timer mechanism often so its springs and gears will not become sluggish.

The self-timer can also be used to reduce camera movement induced by pressing the shutter release. When the self-timer is activated, many seconds elapse before the shutter opens. This allows the camera to settle down from any movement before the shutter opens, especially when the camera is mounted on a tripod or other steadying device. This technique works well for still scenes, however moving subjects cannot be anticipated accurately for use with the self-timer.

ME and ME Super Depth-of-Field Calculation

The ME and ME Super are not equipped with a depth-of-field preview feature. Therefore, depth of field must be calculated with the depth-of-field scale that can be found on virtually every single focal length lens. The most comprehensive depth-of-field guide can be found in a handy little publication, *KODAK Pocket Photoguide,* distributed by Silver Pixel Press. This tiny guide full of photographic field data will fit into any pocket, purse, or gadget bag. The section devoted to depth of field includes a dial that allows anyone to easily compute depth of field for any focal length lens at any aperture.

MX Depth-of-Field Preview Lever

Though there are many charts, scales, and tables available for computing depth of field, seeing it through the viewfinder is often the preferred method when the camera has a depth-of-field preview feature.

The Pentax MX has a depth-of-field preview lever, which also acts as a self-timer lever. When at rest, its tip points to the "X" of "MX" on the camera's face. When the lever is pushed toward the lens and held, depth-of-field preview is activated. This stops the lens down to the actual aperture that will be used when the exposure is made (the "working aperture"). Looking through a viewfinder at the working aperture and interpreting the depth of field is difficult because the further the lens is stopped down, the darker the viewfinder becomes and the harder the image is to see. It takes much patience and practice.

While the lever is engaged, the lens' aperture ring can be rotated to different openings. As the aperture is changed, changes in depth of field can be seen through the viewfinder. Releasing the lever returns the diaphragm to its wide-open position to restore bright viewing.

Basic Flash Operation

The Pentax ME, ME Super, and MX cameras have built-in hot shoes plus PC flash terminals. The hot shoes are located on the top of the pentaprism housing; the PC terminals are located on the side of the lens mount opposite the self-timer lever.

All three models have hot shoes (with an X terminal) that synchronize for electronic flash. The ME and ME Super models have only an X terminal, while the MX contains both an X and an FP outlet. Any terminal marked "FP" should not be used with electronic flash—the FP socket is primarily for flash bulb synchronization.

Most electronic flash units these days make contact through the hot shoe. Few require, or even allow for, synchronization through use of a connecting cord. The most common use for a connecting cord is its ability to move the flash away from the camera, for off-camera flash.

The Pentax ME Super offers basic dedicated flash functions when using dedicated electronic flash units. When a dedicated flash is inserted into the camera's shoe and the flash is ready to fire, it automatically sets the shutter speed to 1/125 second, and a ready light glows in the viewfinder.

When a Pentax ME Super is used with a non-dedicated flash unit, or when a Pentax MX or ME is used with an electronic flash, the shutter speed must be set to X. Electronic flash used at speeds faster than the camera's designated X speed will produce partially exposed frames.

Pentax and other manufacturers have produced countless flash units that will function properly with M-series Pentax cameras, but each model is different and has individual requirements. For best results, consult the flash unit's instruction manual for compatibility and features.

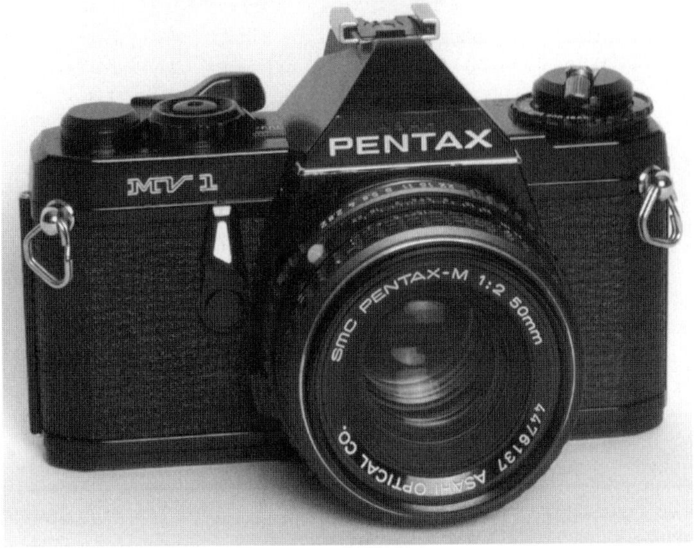

Asahi Pentax MV-1

Pentax MV and MV-1

If a person is familiar with the features and functions of the Pentax ME, ME Super, and MX, the rest of the series is easily decipherable.

Introduced in 1979, the Pentax MV is a greatly simplified version of the Pentax ME. It was designed to appeal to photographers who wanted a simpler version of a high-quality camera. By omitting many features and functions, Pentax produced the MV at a substantially lower price than the ME.

The Pentax MV has the same body and shutter as the ME, but the viewfinder contains minimal exposure data. A green signal light indicates that exposure is correct, usually at a shutter speed of 1/60 or faster, presumed to be fast enough to eliminate camera shake if you are using a normal (50mm) lens. A yellow light means that the exposure is correct, but the camera should be mounted on a tripod or other appropriate support to prevent camera shake if using a normal lens. The light changes from green to yellow at 1/30 second, but there is no way of knowing exactly what shutter

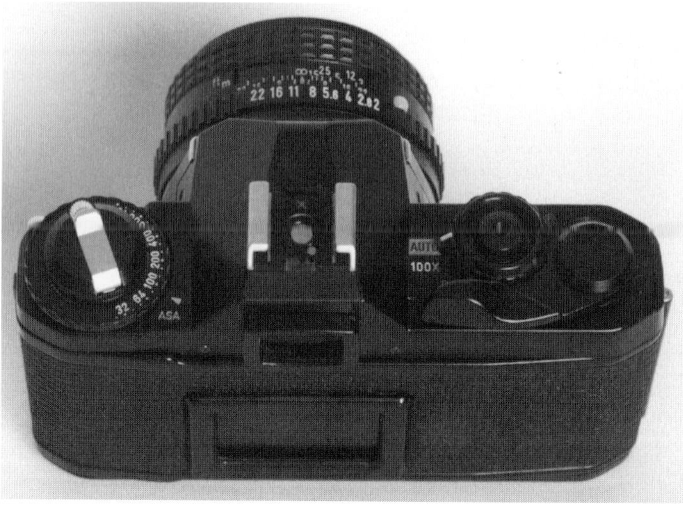

The Pentax MV and MV-1 have only three exposure mode or shutter speed options, AUTO, 100X, and B.

speed the yellow light is indicating. A red light signifies an exposure setting beyond the shutter, lens, or meter's capability.

A ready light ("X") appears below the exposure indicator when any dedicated flash connected to the Pentax MV's hot shoe is ready to fire.

The MV's exposure mode control offers three options: "AUTO" (Automatic mode), "100X" (mechanical shutter speed and flash

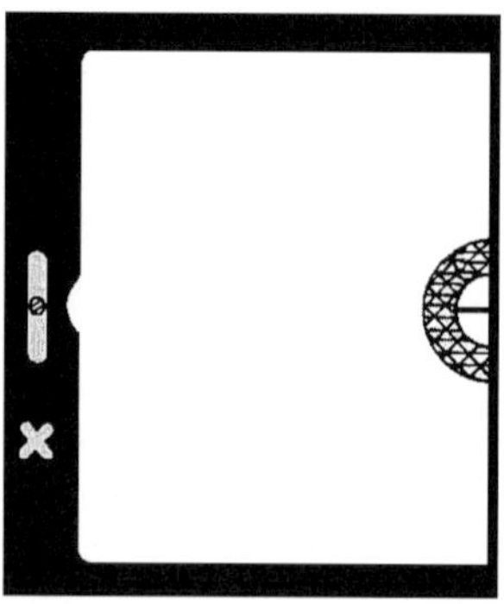

The MV and MV-1's viewfinder display is very simple. The display shows a green LED if the exposure is correct, a yellow LED if the exposure may be subject to camera shake, and a red LED if the exposure is beyond the capabilities of the camera or lens. The X flash ready light illuminates when a dedicated flash is mounted and ready to fire.

sync speed), and "B." These operate the same as on the ME (see pages 93 and 96 for more information). At the time of its manufacture, no one realized that this limited amount of user control would be the way many modern cameras would evolve. In fact, the Pentax MV was in many ways the predecessor to today's point-and-shoot cameras.

The Pentax MV has no way of setting exposure compensation, but exposure compensation can be achieved by altering the film speed setting. An exposure compensation indicator dial located underneath the rewind knob assists the photographer in performing these calculations. Setting the film speed dial to a speed that is twice the actual film rating will cause a 1-stop underexposure correction. Conversely, rating the film at half of its normal speed will yield an exposure that is 1 stop more than the light meter suggests. Naturally, compensation need not be made in full stops; fractional-stop compensation is often the necessary solution.

There are two differences between the Pentax MV and the MV-1 (introduced in 1980). The MV-1 can be used with an accessory winder, while the Pentax MV can not. Also, the MV-1 has a built-in self-timer, while the MV does not.

Pentax MG

Introduced around 1982, the Pentax MG is a camera model that lies somewhere between the Pentax ME and MV. Its exterior controls are similar to the MV's, but its viewfinder information display is like that of the ME.

The MG's exposure mode control dial offers AUTO, 100X, and B, just like the MV. The AUTO setting is Automatic exposure mode, and the 100X setting is the mechanical shutter speed, which can be used if the batteries die unexpectedly. It is also the flash sync speed. B is the bulb speed, which is used for taking long exposures.

The MG has an exposure compensation indicator dial that is concealed underneath the rewind knob. It is visible when the rewind knob is slightly elevated.

***Caution**: Be careful when lifting the rewind knob to set exposure compensation. Lifting it too high will open the camera back, exposing the film.*

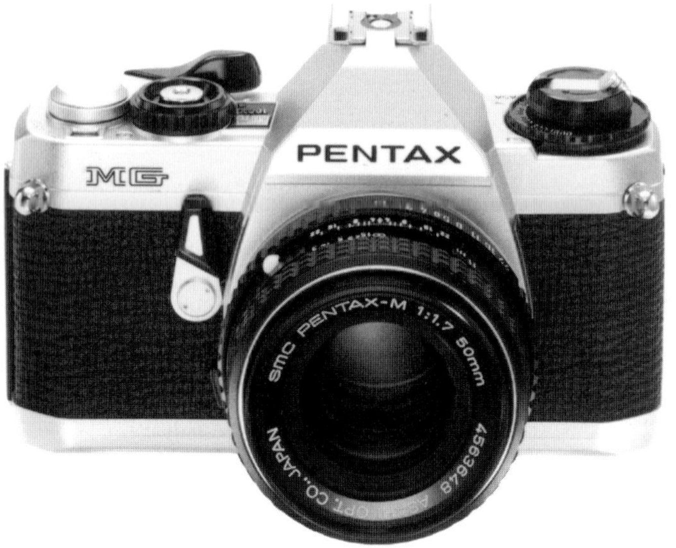

The Pentax MG is an automatic camera made for the photographer who wants simplicity.

The exposure compensation indicator dial is only a visual aid. To use it, turn the top of the dial until the index mark is aligned with the ASA/ISO of the film in use, then lift and turn the ASA/ISO dial until the ASA/ISO rating points to the amount of compensation desired on the inner dial. Each dot on the compensation dial represents 1 full stop; partial-stop compensation is possible by setting an approximate distance between dots.

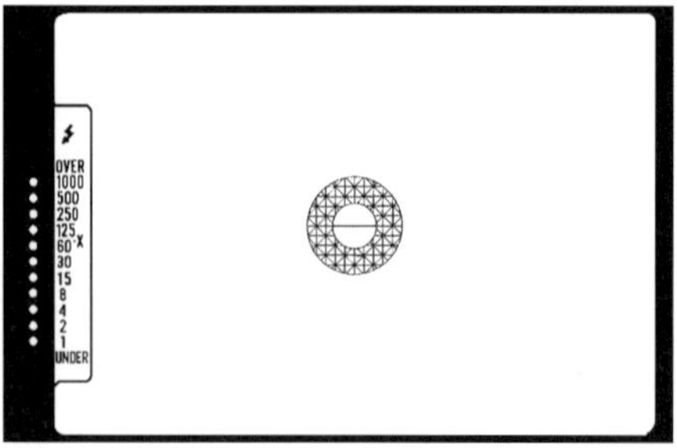

The viewfinder on the Pentax MG displays the camera's shutter speeds, over- and underexposure warnings, and a flash ready light. The selected shutter speed is indicated by an illuminated LED.

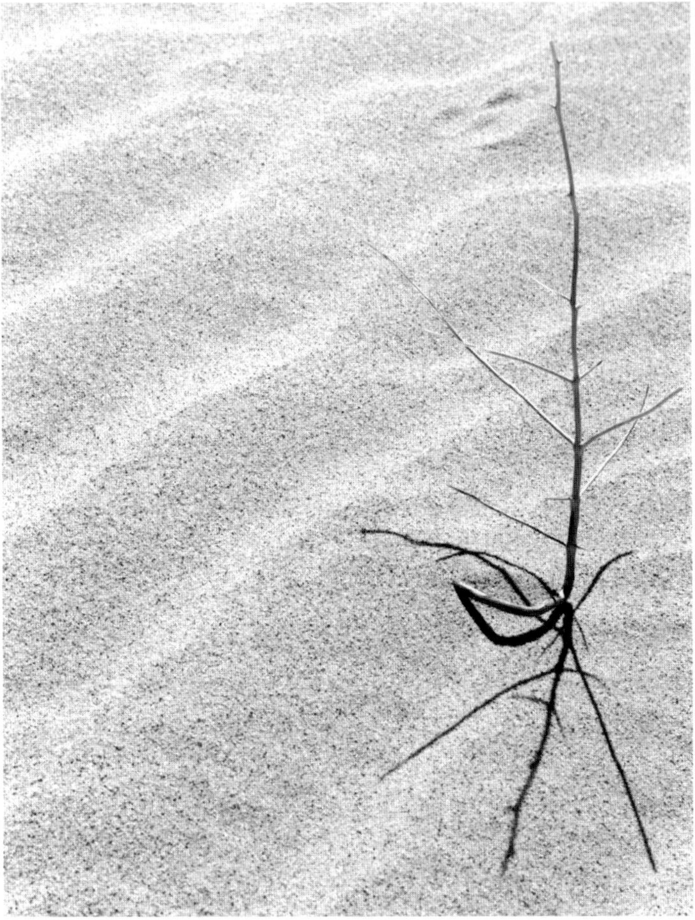

A delicate subject with a uniformly bright background such as this would be difficult to capture using an autoexposure mode. A gray card reading will ensure proper exposure.

The exposure data in the viewfinder of the Pentax MG is much like the corresponding information in the viewfinder of the Pentax ME. The major differences are that the MG contains dedicated flash data, the ME does not; the shutter speed range on the MG is 1 to 1/1000 second, and on the ME it is 8 seconds to 1/1000 second.

At the top of the information strip in the MG's viewfinder is a lightning bolt. When a red LED is lit next to this symbol, a dedicated flash unit is mounted, its capacitor is fully charged, and it is ready to fire.

The two other red LEDs warn of over- or underexposure when they light next to the words "OVER" or "UNDER" respectively. Green LEDs indicate the shutter speed range from 1/1000 second to 1/60 second, theoretically safe for hand-held shooting. Yellow LEDs indicate shutter speeds of 1/30 second to 1 second and warn of potential camera shake. An "X" LED indicates that the shutter has automatically been set to the sync speed of 1/100 second when a dedicated flash unit is being used.

Because the photographer has control over the aperture, he or she can select a desirable aperture-shutter speed combination or an acceptable compromise. (By changing the f/stop, the shutter speed is forced into a corresponding setting for proper exposure.) Also, because the photographer can compensate for exposure using the exposure compensation indicator (adjusting the ASA/ISO setting), a small amount of control is available if desired.

With the Pentax MG you can use one of the Pentax M-series winders; either the ME or ME II winder will drive the MG (see page 172 for more information).

Pentax MEF

The MEF is the final Pentax camera in the M series. Introduced in 1982, it was the camera that ushered in the age of Pentax autofocus SLRs.

The Pentax MEF, for all practical purposes, is a Pentax ME Super with autofocus operation. The exposure control mechanisms and functions on these two cameras are identical. An autofocus control panel, located near the rewind knob, and the additional autofocus data in the viewfinder set the two cameras apart. Another difference can be observed when comparing the lens mounts: The MEF lens mount contains electrical contacts that feed information to the autofocus lens.

Another difference is the MEF's battery compartment—it requires four S76 batteries (or equivalent), twice the number of the other M-series cameras.

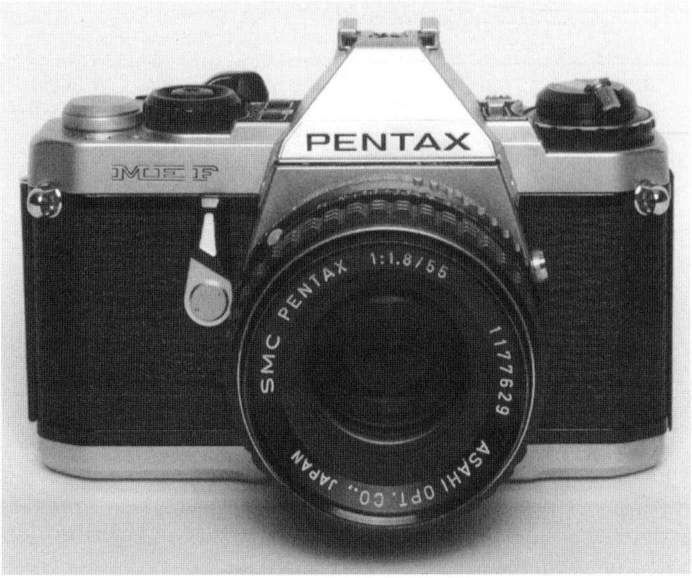

The Pentax MEF was the company's first autofocus SLR camera.

The Pentax MEF was sold with a 35-70mm f/2.8 autofocus lens that contained a built-in autofocus motor. The MEF also functions with conventional K-mount lenses, but is limited to electronically assisted focusing only.

The autofocus control panel, located on the left side of the camera's top plate, contains a switch with three positions. The "off" position disengages the autofocus system, the "red" position is used with lenses that have a maximum aperture of f/3.5 or slower, and the "green" setting is used with lenses that have a maximum aperture of f/2.8 or faster.

At the rear of the autofocus control panel is a switch that activates or silences an audible signal. When this feature is engaged, a tone sounds when sharp focus has been achieved.

The viewfinder of the Pentax MEF contains three autofocus diodes. When the center one is illuminated, the object in the viewfinder's center circle is in focus. On either side of the center diode are two red arrowheads; they indicate the direction that the lens' focusing ring must be turned in order to achieve sharp focus.

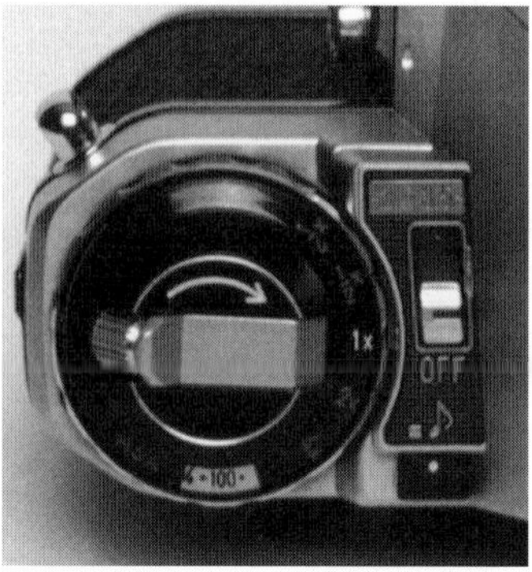

The Pentax MEF's autofocus control panel has a three-position switch that is set to correspond to the speed of the lens in use. Its two-position switch turns on and off the audible focus confirmation signal.

A Pentax MEF focuses automatically when used in conjunction with its unique 35-70mm autofocus zoom lens (not to be confused with the later F-series autofocus lenses). When used with conventional K-mount lenses with apertures of f/5.6 or faster, the Pentax MEF works in the following manner: When the system is activated, one of the three viewfinder autofocus LEDs is illuminated. If a red arrowhead appears, the photographer should turn the lens focusing ring in the direction indicated by the arrow until the center diode lights up to achieve focus. (Some aftermarket lenses will not operate this way.) This electronic focusing assistance means that the photographer need not rely on his or her eyesight to achieve critical focus.

Autofocus systems measure image contrast; the more contrast they see, the better they function. Early autofocus systems, like the Pentax MEF's, are inefficient by today's standards; autofocusing is achieved only under ideal conditions. But virtually no new concept is presented in the marketplace as a fully developed system. Most major camera manufacturers, including Pentax, offered a short-lived incipient autofocusing system in the early days.

The success of the Pentax MEF should not be measured by the length of its production run or by the number of units sold. It is a pioneer, a forerunner, that any serious Pentax camera collector should own.

Each Pentax M-series camera has its own place in history. The intelligence of the people who direct the Asahi Optical Company is evidenced in their ability to capitalize on previous successes. Just as the K-series cameras echoed the Spotmatic family, many modern cameras mirror their M-series predecessors.

Pentax LX

The Pentax LX is considered by most Asahi aficionados to be the finest camera the Asahi Optical Company produced. When it was introduced, everyone in the photographic industry took note. Unlike many other camera models, it entered the marketplace fully developed and remained virtually unmodified during its entire life span. There have been no subsequent Pentax models to replace it.

The LX could be considered a commemorative camera; it was produced to coincide with the Asahi Optical Company's 60th anniversary. The Roman numeral LX doubles as both a commemorative date and the camera's name.

Pentax LX Specifications

Introduced: 1980

Type: 35mm (24 x 36mm format), single-lens-reflex

Lens Mount: Asahi Pentax K bayonet mount

Viewfinder: Interchangeable. Standard FA-1 eyelevel pentaprism finder shows 98% vertical and 95% horizontal view of the picture area. Full-information data display. Built-in diopter corrector.

Focusing Screen: Interchangeable; 14 screens available. Standard SC-21 contains split-image rangefinder, microprism doughnut, and ground-glass field.

Shutter: Electro-mechanical, horizontally traveling, titanium focal plane shutter

Shutter Speeds:

Manual Mechanical: B, plus all speeds on the dial from X (1/75 second) to 1/2000 second. These mechanically controlled speeds function without batteries.

Manual Electronic: From 4 seconds to 1/60 second

Electronic: Stepless, from 125 seconds to 1/2000 second

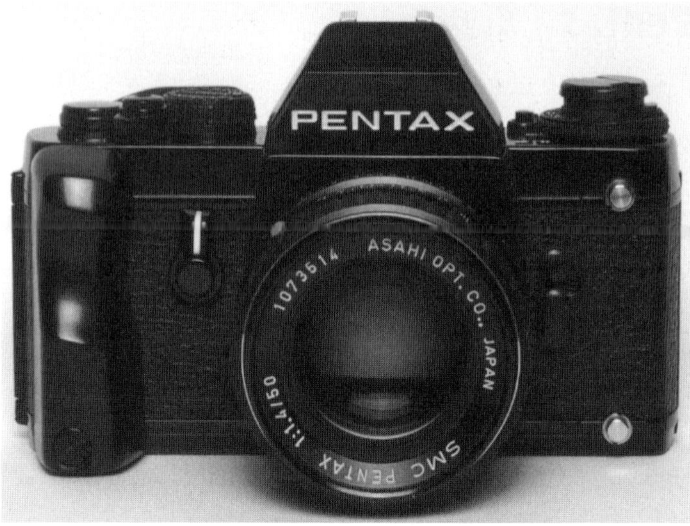

Pentax LX

Film Advance: Manual advance using a single-stroke, rapid-wind lever; 120° throw and 25° stand-off angle. Automatic film advance possible with either the optional Winder LX or Motor Drive LX

Film Rewind: Manual advance using fold-out crank. Power rewind using optional Motor Drive LX or Winder LX.

Exposure Counter: Additive; as exposures are made, counter progresses from 0 to 36. As film is rewound, counter counts down providing accurate tracking for multiple exposures.

Exposure Measurement:

Manual: EV 1 to EV 19

Automatic: EV –6.5 to EV 20

Exposure Compensation: +/– 2 stops in 1/3-stop increments

Self-Timer/Depth-of-Field Preview/ Mirror Lock-up:	Multi-function lever provides shutter delay (4 to 10 seconds), depth-of-field preview, or mirror lock.
Flash Control:	TTL metering with properly dedicated flash units; ready light and exposure confirmation visible in viewfinder.
Flash Synchronization:	FP and X sync terminals. FP flash terminal on the camera's face; X terminal on the camera's face and hot shoe.
Power Source:	Two 1.5v S76 batteries, or equivalent
Dimensions (without lens)*:	1.9 D x 3.6 H x 5.7″W (50 x 90.5 x 144.5 mm)
Weight*:	20.1 oz. (570 g)

**Weight and size measurements are with the standard FA-1 finder.*

Using the Pentax LX

Battery Installation and Testing

The Pentax LX takes two 1.5v S76-type batteries, or equivalent. To check battery voltage, activate the camera's metering system by partially depressing the shutter release button. While looking through the viewfinder, observe the shutter speed LED. A continuous glow indicates adequate battery voltage, weak batteries will cause the LED to flicker, and dead batteries will not illuminate the diodes. At the first sign of trouble, replace the batteries.

"Batteryless" Camera Operation

The LX camera incorporates an electro-mechanical shutter mechanism, which enables the photographer to take pictures over a wide range of shutter speeds when the batteries are exhausted or removed from the camera. The mechanical shutter speeds are B, X (1/75 second), and any speed faster than X (1/125, 1/250, 1/500, 1/1000, and 1/2000).

If battery failure occurs while the camera is in the Automatic exposure mode, or if it occurs when the shutter speed is set at 1/60 second or slower, the mirror will lock in the "up" position. To

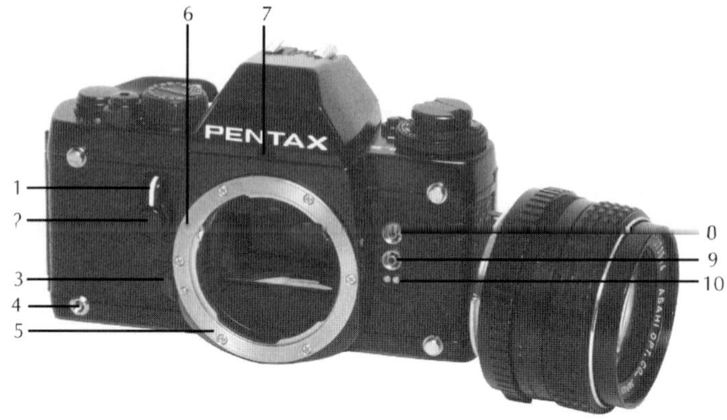

1. **Self-timer/Depth-of-field preview/Mirror lock lever**
2. **Lever release button**
3. **Lens release**
4. **Grip mounting socket**
5. **Lens mount**
6. **Lens mounting index**
7. **Aperture readout window**
8. **FP flash sync terminal**
9. **X flash sync terminal**
10. **Auto flash contacts**

release the mirror, set the shutter release dial to any mechanically operated speed.

Viewfinder Installation and Removal

Only the most sophisticated cameras offer interchangeable viewfinders. The Pentax LX falls into this category with eight optional viewfinders. Upon purchasing the camera new, the photographer could choose whichever finder he or she wanted. See page 179 for more information.

To remove the viewfinder from the camera body, move the finder release lever counterclockwise, then slide the finder toward the back of the camera and remove. Slide a new finder onto the camera body, reversing the above procedure. Do not engage the finder release lever; it is used for prism removal only. When the prism is in place, a click will be heard and felt. Then, for safety's sake, try to slide the prism to the rear *without* using the release lever. This final step ensures that the prism will not fall off accidentally.

Caution is required when removing any camera component. Before removing a viewfinder, make sure there is a clean, dry, and

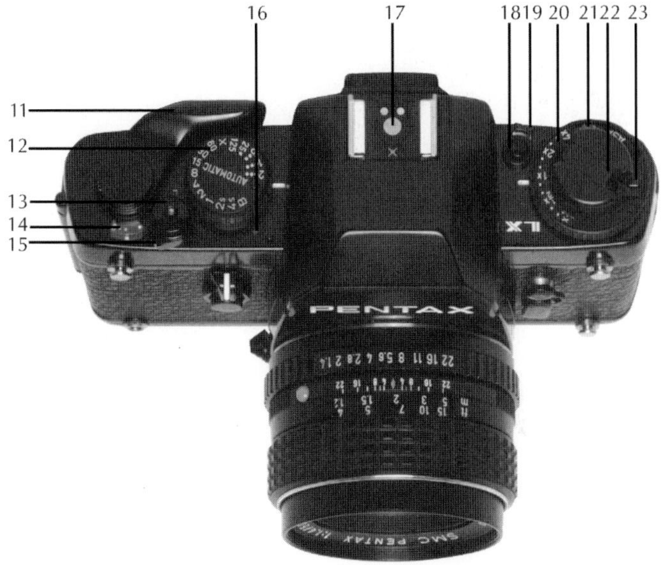

11. **Film advance lever**
12. **Shutter speed dial**
13. **Shutter release button**
14. **Frame counter**
15. **Shutter lock**
16. **Shutter-cocked indicator**
17. **Accessory hot shoe**
18. **Shutter speed dial lock release button**
19. **Finder release lever**
20. **Exposure compensation dial**
21. **ASA/ISO window**
22. **Film rewind crank**
23. **ASA/ISO dial lock release button**

non-abrasive place to put it. Avoid changing finders, lenses, and rolls of film in windy, dusty environments, if possible.

Diopter Adjustment

The Pentax FA-1, FA-1W, FD-1, FE-1, and FA-2 viewfinders contain built-in diopter correcting mechanisms. Most photographers can adjust these finders themselves to correct for any eye-focusing deficiency they may have.

To adjust the diopter setting on the FA-1, FA-1W, and FA-2, partially remove the prism, sliding it back just enough to expose the diopter adjustment screw at the rear of the prism below the eyepiece. (While doing this procedure, take care because the prism

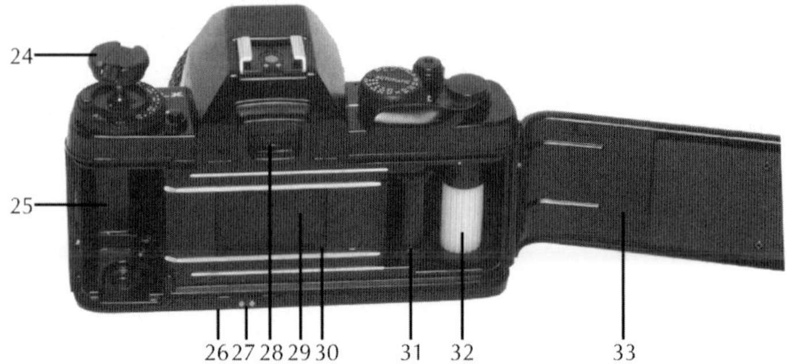

24. Film back release knob
25. Film chamber
26. Battery chamber (on base of camera)
27. Data back contacts
28. Viewfinder eyepiece
29. Shutter
30. Dial data blind
31. Film sprocket
32. Film take-up spool
33. Back cover

is no longer locked in place.) With the prism in this position, look at the split-image spot in the center of the viewfinder. Adjust the screw using the tool supplied with the finder until the split-image lines are sharp and clear. When the best possible diopter adjustment has been achieved, remove the tool, reposition the finder, and lock the finder into place. Again verify that the finder is securely locked in place as described above.

The Pentax FD-1 and FE-1 viewfinders contain externally adjustable diopter-correcting helical focusing rings. Diopter adjustment is made with a simple turn of the ring.

Note: Diopter adjustments are made by focusing your eye on the dark lines on the finder screen, not the image seen by the camera.

Loading Film

The first step in loading film should be to set the shutter speed dial to a fast speed. Film should be loaded in subdued light. An LX shutter speed dial set to Automatic mode and with the lens cap on will result in a long shutter speed while the film is being advanced and may lead you to believe the shutter has jammed. Therefore, a fast manual shutter speed is recommended.

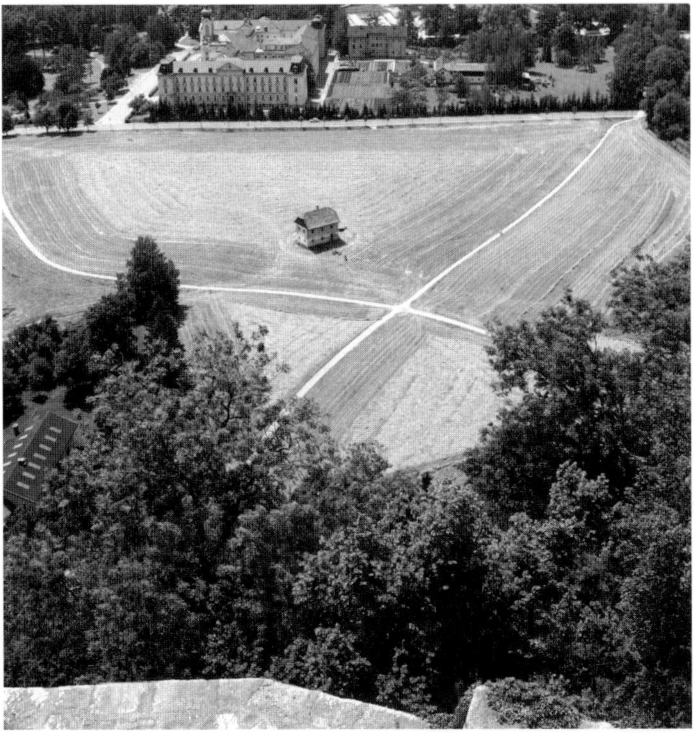

Automatic exposure mode is ideal for a scene such as this with a balance of light and dark areas. The only thing required is to set a small aperture for extensive depth of field, and the camera will set the corresponding shutter speed for proper exposure.

Advancing Film

The LX film advance lever is a single-stroke rapid-wind lever. It requires 120° of throw to advance the film and cock the shutter. The lever also has a 25° stand-off position, which makes it easy to find; the photographer can be looking through the viewfinder and concentrating on the events at hand while advancing the film.

The shutter-cocked indicator (located just in front of the shutter speed dial) turns red when the shutter is cocked; the red disappears when the shutter is not cocked.

Exposure Counter

Located just in front of the film advance lever is the frame counter, which advances one frame each time the film advance lever is wound. The counter resets itself to zero (0) each time the camera back is opened. The numbers "0," "20," "24," and "36" are marked in red. The counter also works in reverse; when the film is being rewound, the film counter accurately counts down. This feature can be helpful when making multiple exposures.

Setting the Film Speed

To set the film speed, press the ASA/ISO dial-lock release and turn the dial until the desired film speed rating is opposite the index mark. Make sure that the film speed dial has clicked into a "click stop." A slight twist of the dial will ensure that it is locked in place.

Memo Holder

On the back of the LX is a memo holder, which is sized to contain the end of a film carton or other important hand-written notes. This can help remind you of the film type loaded, number of exposures, or other important exposure data you might need.

Focusing Screens

Most manually focused SLRs with split-image or microprism focusing aids focus in approximately the same way, and the Pentax LX is no exception. However, the LX is one of the few early Pentax models that offer user-interchangeable focusing screens, so different focusing techniques can be used. The Pentax LX offers 14 interchangeable focusing screens, so you can select and change screens to match any shooting situation. (See page 178 for more information.)

To change an LX focusing screen, select a clean, dry, dust-free environment. When handling screens, remember there will be two screens outside the camera, and both will need a clean, safe place to rest.

Caution: *Exercise great caution when handling focusing screens—they are etched, ground, or scored plastic—and very easily scratched! Once scratched, they are damaged forever; the scratches cannot be polished out.*

Access to the focusing screens is gained through the camera's lens cavity. Each interchangeable screen comes with a special pair of tweezers. Insert the tweezers' nose against the top plate of the mount, resting the tweezers in the indentation located in the screen's mounting plate. Lift the handle of the tweezers in a gentle upward motion. The focusing screen frame will drop down, exposing the screen and its handling tab.

Once its frame has been lowered, grab the screen's tab with the tweezer jaws, remove the screen, and place it in a storage container. To install the new screen, use the tweezers to grab the tab, insert the screen into the camera's screen frame, and push the frame back to its original locked position.

Note: Remember, changing screens must be done with care. If the screen frame does not release immediately, do not exert pressure. The screen or the camera's mirror can easily become scratched with just a slip of the wrist.

Shutter Speed Dial

The shutter speed dial allows photographers to select their choice of shutter speeds, from B to 1/2000 second. "B" stands for bulb, which keeps the shutter open as long as the shutter release button is depressed. "4s," "2s," and "1s" refer to 4 seconds, 2 seconds, and 1 second, respectively. Numbers higher than 1 refer to fractions of a second (2 is 1/2 second, 15 is 1/15 second, etc.). On the LX, "X" is 1/75 second, the sync speed for electronic flash.

The locking detent marked "AUTOMATIC" is also located on the shutter speed dial. With the dial set in this position, the camera's electronics choose the exposure. Today Automatic mode is referred to as Aperture-Preferred or Aperture-Priority mode.

The Pentax LX's shutter speed dial locks in the AUTOMATIC position. To set a speed other than AUTOMATIC, depress the shutter speed dial lock release button while turning the dial.

The Pentax LX's shutter can be controlled mechanically or electronically. The mechanical speeds are from 1/2000 second to X and B. These speeds do not require battery power; springs and gears do the timing. Should your batteries fail, all camera functions except light meter related operations are usable.

Electronic shutter speed control allows for a wide range of speeds in the Automatic mode. In this mode the electronically controlled speeds are stepless, ranging from 125 seconds to 1/2000 second.

In Manual mode, the electronically controlled shutter speeds are not stepless, ranging from 1/60 second to 4 seconds, and all shutter speeds faster than 1/60 second are mechanically controlled.

Shutter Release Lock

The shutter release lock encircles the shutter release button and does exactly what its name implies. If the shutter is cocked, this "safety" can be engaged, preventing accidental exposures. Sliding it to the left locks the shutter release and disables the metering system, and sliding it to the right unlocks the shutter release button and all its functions.

Light Meter Activation

The light meter can be activated in one of two ways: either by pressing the shutter release button partway, or for special applications, by depressing the exposure compensation dial lock release.

Note: Early versions of the Pentax LX did not include the latter feature unless specially modified.

Partially depress the shutter release button to turn on the light meter. Once activated, the meter will remain on for 25 seconds, after which a battery-conserving mechanism will turn the meter off.

When a motor drive or winder is attached to the Pentax LX, the shutter release stroke is extremely short; accidental exposures often result when checking exposure by using the shutter release button if a drive unit is attached. When the camera has one of these accessories attached, it is advisable to check meter functions through the exposure compensation dial lock release button.

Viewfinder Exposure Data

When you look into the viewfinder of a Pentax LX, you'll see more than the scene and the focusing screen. Displayed in the borders of the scene are useful data. Centered at the top of the finder is the aperture setting.

The information panel running along the right side of the finder, from top to bottom, informs the photographer of the following data:

Most Pentax LX viewfinders include all pertinent exposure information: selected aperture, manually selected shutter speed, meter's recommended shutter speed, Automatic exposure mode, exposure compensation warning, slow shutter speed warning (to forewarn you of the possibility of camera shake), and flash ready light.

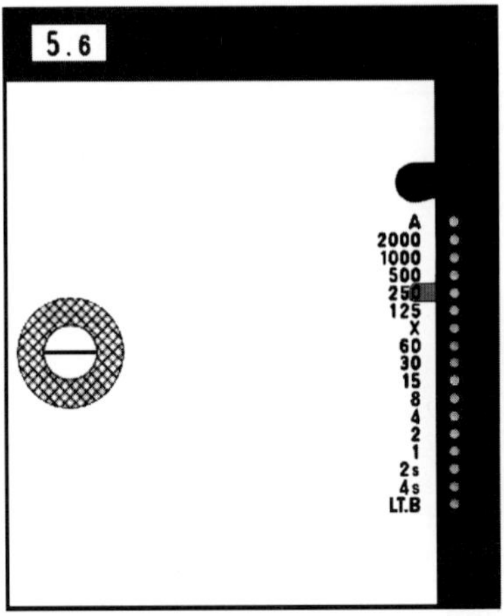

Red flag Exposure compensation has been set.
Blue flag Selected shutter speed
Red LED Overexposure warning
A Automatic exposure mode selected
Green LED Shutter speed from 1/30 to 1/2000 second selected. Generally safe for hand-held shooting with a 50mm lens.
X Sync speed (1/75 second) for electronic flash. Glows red to indicate flash is charged and ready when camera is used with dedicated flash unit.
Yellow LED Shutter speed of 1/15 second to 4 seconds selected. A tripod or other steadying device is recommended.
LT.B In Automatic mode, indicates Long Time exposure; in Manual mode, indicates B.

Automatic Exposure Control

When the shutter speed dial is set to AUTOMATIC, the camera selects the shutter speed that it believes will yield the best exposure when combined with the photographer's selected aperture. Some of the variables that affect its decision are lighting conditions and film speed.

The Pentax LX's Automatic mode is today referred to as Aperture-Preferred or Aperture-Priority mode. The photographer selects the aperture, and the camera selects the shutter speed.

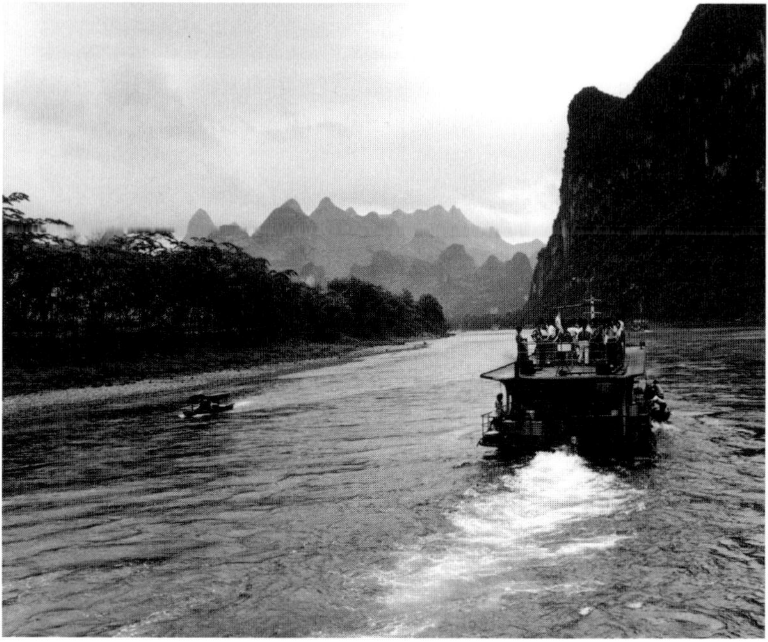

The beautiful Li River in China presents breathtaking vistas at every turn. Wise photographers are always prepared for once-in-a-lifetime shots; Automatic exposure mode is ideal in these situations.

This is the mode of choice when a photographer wants automatic exposure selection but does not wish to relinquish complete control. When the Pentax LX is held, it is more convenient to change the aperture than turn the shutter speed dial. By changing the aperture, the photographer can indirectly select a desired shutter speed. The changing shutter speed and aperture can be observed by looking at the viewfinder display. Practice with the camera in different hypothetical shooting situations.

To operate the LX in Automatic mode, first set the shutter speed dial to AUTOMATIC. The dial will lock in that position and the A in the viewfinder will be encircled by the blue flag. Next, select an appropriate aperture, and shoot.

In Automatic mode, the camera selects the shutter speed, which is indicated by an LED in the viewfinder display. (In the stepless speed range, the LED will indicate the nearest nominal speed.) As stated earlier, changing the f/stop causes the camera to select another shutter speed.

When the camera is set to the Automatic mode, various LEDs will light depending on the situation:

A red LED will glow next to the A on the scale when overexposure is probable. Try stopping the lens down or use a light-reducing filter.

A red LED will glow next to the LT.B when the camera has selected a shutter speed longer than 4 seconds, indicating a long time exposure in Automatic mode.

A green LED will glow next to the shutter speed that the camera has selected within the range of 1/30 to 1/2000 second.

Yellow LEDs indicate the shutter speeds selected by the camera within the range of 1/15 second and 4 seconds. At these speeds, camera shake is likely with a 50mm lens, and some form of camera support is recommended; at the slower speeds, a tripod and cable release should definitely be used.

***Caution**: If the camera is in Automatic mode and the shutter is tripped when no light (or very little light) can strike the light meter cell, a long exposure will result. The photographer may even think the camera has jammed. To unlock the shutter, move the shutter release dial to any manual shutter speed setting. After the system returns to normal, the camera may be reset to the mode or speed of choice.*

Manual Exposure Control

The Pentax LX is easy to use in Manual exposure mode. To set a manual shutter speed, press the shutter speed dial lock release, then turn the shutter speed dial from AUTOMATIC to any speed by aligning the speed with the index. The viewfinder's blue flag will encircle the same shutter speed number. Then select the aperture. The selected aperture will appear at the top of the viewfinder.

When depth of field is critical, you should first select the lens aperture—a wide aperture produces shallow depth of field, and a narrow aperture produces extensive depth of field. Next, activate the meter by lightly pressing the shutter release button and note the camera's shutter speed recommendation (indicated by an illuminated LED next to it) in the viewfinder display. If the shutter

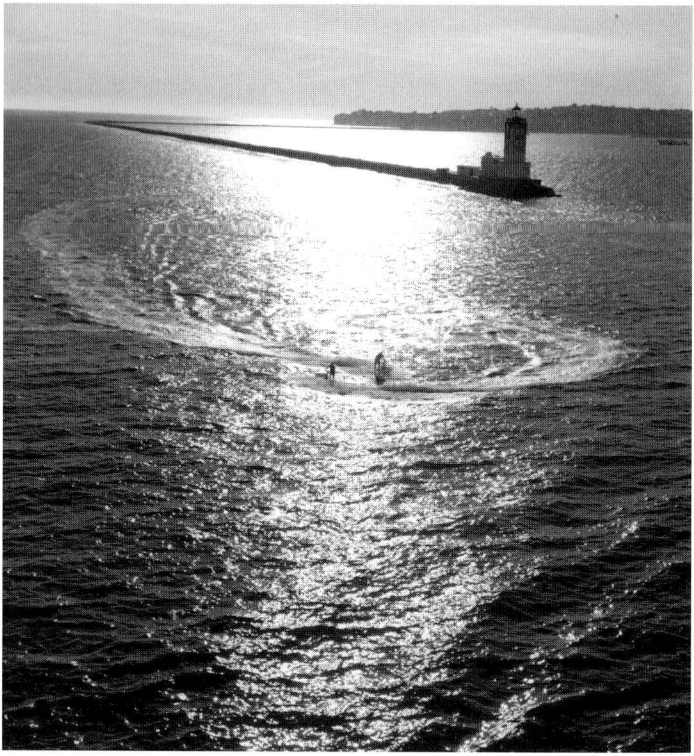

The Pentax LX offers the photographer the option to use Automatic exposure mode or Manual mode. In situations like this, you don't necessarily want to use the meter's recommended reading for the best exposure.

speed recommended is satisfactory, turn the shutter speed dial until the blue flag and LED both indicate the same shutter speed. If everything else is satisfactory, press firmly on the shutter release button and make the exposure.

When freezing action or introducing motion is important to your image, use Manual exposure mode, but first select the shutter speed that will create the desired effect—a faster shutter speed will tend to freeze action, a slower one will tend to blur action. Activate the meter by lightly pressing the shutter release button, and while looking through the viewfinder turn the lens' aperture ring until the viewfinder's illuminated LED indicates the same shutter speed that is encircled by the blue flag.

Usually, when the photographer has opted for the manual method of determining correct exposure, it is because he or she mistrusts the camera's ability to determine correct exposure. The photographer usually wants to control the exposure settings to produce a creative effect or override the camera's metered exposure recommendation. Some photographers use Manual mode often, and some use it only for special applications. Keep in mind that matching the exposure settings to the camera's metered exposure when in Manual mode does nothing more than replicate an exposure that could have been more easily made in Automatic mode.

Exposure Compensation

The exposure compensation dial is located beneath the film rewind knob. It allows the photographer to bias the camera's automatic exposure setting in 1/3-stop increments by +/– 2 f/stops. The normal position for this dial is at the 1x detent. When the exposure compensation dial is not at its normal position, a red warning flag appears in the viewfinder display.

The exposure compensation range is not always 2 full stops. When using ISO 6 film, for instance, the compensation range is 1x, 1/2x, and 1/4x; with ISO 12 film, the range is 2x, 1x, 1/2x, and 1/4x. When using ISO 1600 film, restrictions occur in the other direction, and possible compensations are 4x, 2x, 1x, and 1/2x. ISO 3200 film can be compensated in the range of 4x, 2x, and 1x.

Most photographers, with some experience, can guess when an automatic exposure system will produce unsatisfactory results. Knowing exactly how much compensation is required is a slowly acquired skill (or is it an art?). Many photographers would be better served by an alternate method of exposure determination, such as Manual exposure mode; but if exposure compensation is the correction method of choice, back it up by bracketing, taking several exposures at various settings.

Multiple Exposures

To make a double exposure, take the first exposure the conventional way. Then press the rewind button located on the bottom of the camera to disengage the film advance mechanism and frame counter. Next cock the shutter by winding the film advance lever once. Now trip the shutter to make the second exposure. Each time the film advance lever is swung through its complete arc, the counter and advance mechanism are reengaged to prevent the camera from remaining in the multiple exposure mode. Therefore, if you wish to make additional exposures on the same frame, repeat the above procedure before each exposure. Depending on the effect you are pursuing, some exposure compensation may be necessary due to overlapping image densities.

The Pentax LX also allows you to rewind the film to any already exposed frame on the currently loaded roll, so you can overlay subsequent exposures onto existing ones. However, Asahi claims a 0.2 mm tolerance when rewound multiple exposures are attempted, therefore precise multiple-image alignment should not be expected.

Here is how to accomplish a rewound multiple exposure: First, set the shutter speed dial to a mechanical shutter speed (1/125 second or faster is recommended). Next, depress the film rewind button, and rewind the film until the frame counter reads one number less than the frame you wish to double-expose. Then, cover the lens with a light-tight lens cap. Cock and trip the shutter. The counter now displays the frame number on which the multiple exposure will take place. Remove the lens cover, press the film rewind button, cock the shutter, and make the double exposure.

If you wish to continue making multiple exposures on the same frame, repeat the above procedure. If you wish to double-expose subsequent frames, merely advance the film, and take a second exposure over the previously exposed frames. When you're ready to advance to a frame that has not yet been exposed, select a fast mechanical shutter speed, cover the lens, and advance the film until the counter displays one frame number higher than the last one exposed.

The random access frame counter on the Pentax LX makes all this possible. Because of this feature, photographers can take a series of shots at dusk, for instance, rewind the film to the beginning of the series, install a telephoto lens, and add a moon to each scene after dark.

Mirror Lock-up Lever

The mirror lock-up lever is a multi-function lever—it is a self-timer, depth-of-field preview, and mirror lock-up lever. It is the only lever on the camera face. The Pentax LX's mirror can be locked in the "up" position to reduce vibration caused by mirror bounce. Usually employed while attempting high-magnification photography, this function causes the viewfinder to go dark while it is engaged, therefore, precise framing must be done before the mirror is locked up.

To lock the mirror up, press the lever release button while moving the self-timer/mirror lock-up lever clockwise towards the lens. Remember to press the lever release button; if you do not press the button, moving the lever clockwise will result in depth-of-field preview. To return the mirror to its normal working position, press the lever release button.

Self-Timer

To use the self-timer, press the lever release button and turn the self-timer lever counterclockwise, away from the lens. Select the desired time delay from 4 to 10 seconds. When the self-timer lever is cocked, trip the shutter release button to start the countdown. Should you change your mind before the shutter release button has been depressed, the self-timer can be deactivated. Override the self-timer by returning the lever to its "at-rest" position. Once the shutter release button has been depressed, however, the self-timer sequence is impossible to stop.

Depth-of-Field Preview

Depth-of-field at any aperture can be observed through the viewfinder by pushing the self-timer lever clockwise towards the lens. With the lever in this position, you can change the lens aperture and preview the effect it has on the depth of field. Although practice is required to be able to judge depth of field accurately using this function, once perfected, this skill becomes invaluable. When the lever is released, the aperture returns to its wide-open position for bright viewing.

Tripod Spacer

The Pentax LX comes supplied with a tripod spacer, which is necessary when it is used in conjunction with a large-diameter lens. Because the camera body is so small, some lenses actually interfere with the camera-tripod connection. The tripod spacer that originally came with the camera is easily lost, so a better idea is to use a good quick-coupling device such as the Stroboframe

Camera Auto Quick Release. It will solve the spacing problem and eliminate fumbling when you are mounting or removing the camera from a tripod.

Electronic Flash with the Pentax LX

TTL Flash Metering

When used with a TTL flash, the Pentax LX is capable of through-the-lens flash metering. Naturally, it is also capable of performing any of the less-sophisticated flash functions, such as Automatic or Manual flash mode.

Pentax and many other suppliers have manufactured flash units that are dedicated to the Pentax LX. Fortunately, all Pentax cameras that require dedicated flash units have the same dedication requirements. Even the newer units manufactured to work in conjunction with autofocus cameras function properly with the Pentax LX. If the flash unit's foot matches the terminal configuration of the camera's hot shoe, they are most likely compatible.

Asahi calls their LX TTL metering system Integrated Direct Metering, or "IDM." The TTL metering system allows for an exposure determination of both flash and/or ambient light. This means the IDM measures all light regardless of the source and ensures the best possible exposure. Should the flash fail (the capacitor is not fully charged, the maximum distance is exceeded, etc.) the system will default to non-flash Automatic exposure mode.

To operate the LX in the TTL flash metering mode, set the camera's shutter speed dial to AUTOMATIC, and the flash unit's control setting device to TTL. It's just that simple! The system will work automatically, yield a proper exposure, and confirm that the exposure was correct.

When the photographer switches the flash to the "on" position, the camera sets itself to the sync speed of 1/75 second and illuminates the "X" LED when the unit is fully charged. If the ready light comes on slowly or does not come on at all, check the batteries in both the flash unit and camera.

A dedicated TTL flash unit will also confirm proper exposure. After the exposure has been completed, a blinking LED next to the X on the viewfinder display indicates that the film has received an adequate amount of light. Flash confirmation takes time and battery power, and it is not compatible with rapid-sequence flash photography. Most flashes have a confirmation on/off switch if you wish to disengage this feature.

Some flash units, especially aftermarket ones, are not totally dedicated—they may contain most, but not all, dedicated flash functions. For exact specifications, consult the flash unit's instruction manual. If a manual is not available, or it does not detail its exact functions, try testing the flash with your camera (use good film to judge the results fairly) or ask your local camera store for help. Most have knowledgeable personnel who can answer your questions.

Non-Dedicated Flash Photography

The Pentax LX will produce excellent results when used with non-dedicated flash units. However, more knowledge is required to use a manual flash, and an automatic flash is not as foolproof as a dedicated unit. A non-dedicated flash will not set the shutter automatically to the proper flash sync speed. The photographer must manually select a speed of X or slower; failure to do so will result in frames that are partially exposed or nearly blank.

Next, the aperture appropriate for the subject's distance must be selected. Automatic flash units often allow the photographer to select one f/stop for most typical shots; manual flash units require you to change the aperture for each change in subject distance. For exact operating procedure, consult the flash unit's instruction manual or seek help from your local camera store. If you do not understand how flash units of this type operate, do not attempt to figure them out on your own. The trial and error results will be sporadic as the variables are endless.

Asahi/Pentax Lenses

Before one can fully understand how the family of Asahi lenses evolved, a step back in history is necessary. What worldwide trends were in vogue? What were competitive manufacturers offering? These, and many other factors, influenced decisions made by Asahi.

When the Japanese photo industry was making itself known to the rest of the world, German camera manufacturers controlled the major market share, especially the high-end market. American camera manufacturers were still producing cameras, but mostly low- and medium-priced equipment. Eastman Kodak's better 35mm cameras were manufactured in their Stuttgart, Germany, factory. The high-quality cameras manufactured in the USA were mainly medium- and large-format cameras. Soon, even that market would become an off-shore industry segment.

Early Japanese cameras tended to be copies of German cameras. Nikon copied Contax; Canon copied Leica. When SLRs started to play a bigger part in the overall picture, most Japanese manufacturers looked again to Germany.

The most popular 35mm SLR of the early days was the Exakta, but it was fighting two virtually insurmountable problems—lenses and location. When Exakta manufacturers selected its lens-mounting system, they did not anticipate the range of interchangeable SLR lenses to come. The small diameter of the lens-mounting orifice precluded the adaptation of modern optics to the Exakta bayonet mount. The other problem facing its popularity was that the Exakta factory was located in what was then East Germany. Eastern bloc goods were poorly distributed, considered inferior, and too slowly updated.

Other German 35mm SLR manufacturers seemed to be standardizing their lens-mounting system. Pentacon, Praktica, and Contax SLRs appeared with a 42mm screw mount.

In 1958, after a false start with a non-standard lens mount, Asahi Optical adopted the universal 42mm screw mount. They strategized that by doing so, they could sell their lenses to owners of the other cameras that used this universal screw mount, and

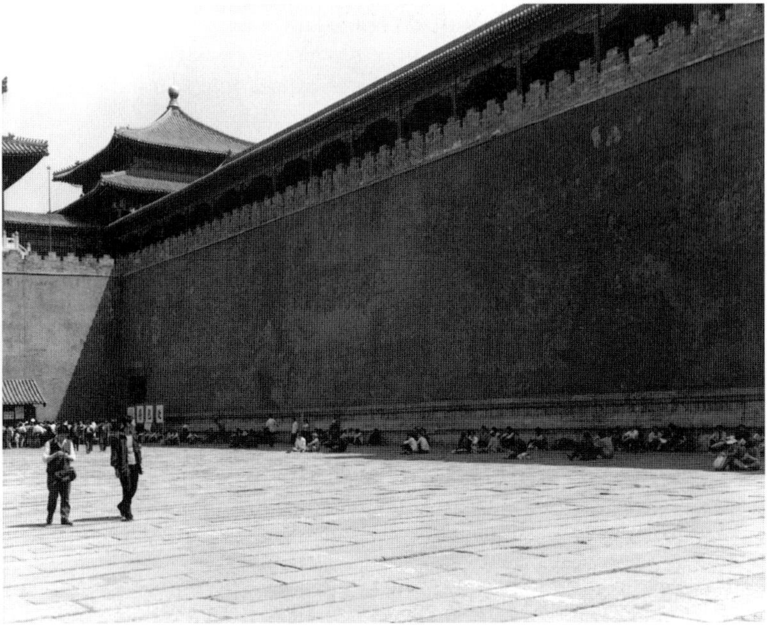

A "normal" lens (50mm on a 35mm SLR) is a powerful tool, as it reproduces the scene as we see it. Normal lenses are sometimes considered "out of vogue" by photographers who prefer to use lenses that render subjects from a different perspective, but these lenses have great potential. With a little imagination, you can use them to create dramatic shots like this.

they could entice photographers who already had screw-mount lenses to purchase Asahi cameras. Asahi became successful with its cameras, lenses, and sales techniques, which earned them worldwide acceptance. Soon the German-designed lens mount became known as the "Pentax Mount." When Asahi introduced its bayonet lens mount, photographers differentiated the two mounts by calling the older the "Pentax Screw Mount," and the newer, "Pentax K Mount." The latter is sometimes referred to as the "Pentax Bayonet Mount," or just the "K Mount."

As photography became simpler for the photographer and more complicated for the camera manufacturer, lenses for Pentax cameras evolved. A knowledgeable observer can determine some important characteristics by a Pentax lens' name. First, let's consider what the names of various screw-mount Asahi-manufactured lenses can tell us, then we will see how their functional changes affected their use.

Asahi Screw-Mount Lenses

All the Asahi-manufactured screw-mount lenses were called Takumar lenses. It has been said that they were named in honor of the Japanese painter, Takuma Kajiwara.

Takumar Lenses

Introduced in 1952, Takumar lenses contained either a manual or a preset diaphragm. A manual diaphragm is just what its name implies—when set, the iris remains there until it is changed. This type of diaphragm is the slowest and most difficult to use.

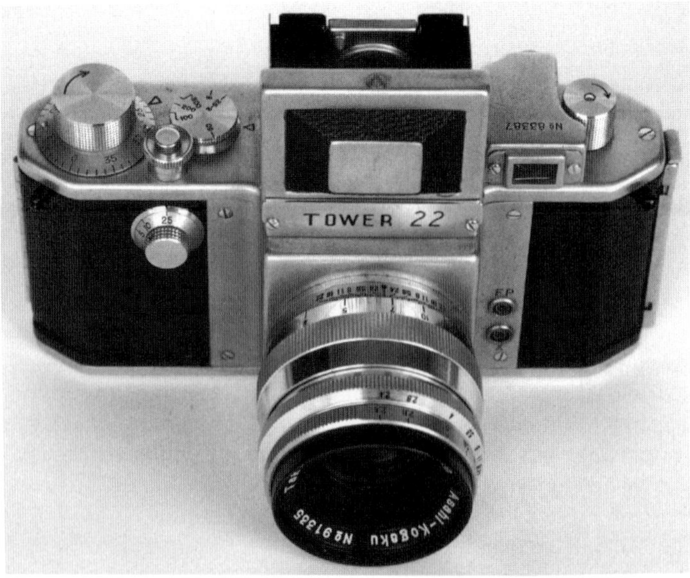

The Tower 22 (also marketed as the Asahiflex IIA) was introduced in 1955 and sold with either a 50mm f/3.5 or a 58mm f/2.4 Takumar lens.

To use a lens with a manual diaphragm, the photographer focuses and composes with the lens wide open, stops the iris down to the required setting, makes the exposure, and then manually sets the aperture back to its maximum opening in preparation for composing the next shot (at the widest aperture, the viewfinder is at its brightest, allowing for easier composition and focusing).

A lens with a preset diaphragm is somewhat easier to use, as the photographer doesn't have to take the camera away from his or her eye to stop the lens down to the taking aperture. These lenses contain two aperture rings, a conventional, "active" ring and a preset ring. To use the preset feature, the photographer sets the preset ring to the desired taking aperture while leaving the conventional ring set at the lens' maximum aperture to compose and focus the image. Before tripping the shutter, the photographer simply turns the conventional aperture ring until it stops; the preset ring stops the conventional ring at the desired, preset setting.

Auto-Takumar Lenses

In 1958, Asahi introduced lenses with "automatic" diaphragms that today we would call "semi-automatic." Auto-Takumar lenses contain an iris-cocking lever. When the photographer selects an aperture, the lens stops down to that setting. But cocking the lever causes the iris blades to open fully. When the shutter release button is tripped, just before the shutter opens, the iris closes down to the set aperture. The iris remains at that setting until it is changed manually or the lever is cocked again.

Super-Takumar Lenses

In 1963, lenses with fully automatic diaphragms were available for Pentax cameras, which at the time were the Spotmatics. Because Asahi used the name Auto-Takumar prematurely, the name Super-Takumar was coined for these lenses. An automatic diaphragm allows the photographer to select an aperture, view the subject through a wide-open lens, shoot at the selected aperture, and then see the subject again at full aperture as soon as the mirror has returned to its resting position. Basically, the lens remains open for viewing purposes, stopping down only at the instant of exposure. This auto-diaphragm mechanism could be overridden for a visual depth-of-field preview.

It is hard to imagine today the impact that the invention of the automatic diaphragm had on photography in the 1960s. Photographic equipment changed more radically in the following decades than it did in the entire first century of its existence.

Takumar Lenses for Photography Beyond the Visible Spectrum

In the years between 1967 and 1975 Pentax produced three special-application lenses for photographing ultraviolet (UV) and/or infrared light: the Quartz-Takumar 85mm f/3.5 (ca. 1967), the Ultra-Achromatic Takumar 85mm f/4.5, and the Ultra-Achromatic Takumar 300mm f/5.6 (both ca. 1970–1975). Although Pentax had not coined the term "Ultra-Achromatic" at the time they came out with the Quartz-Takumar lens, it nevertheless belongs in that category. Ultraviolet photography is used by criminologists to detect forged checks, altered documents, blood stains, and fingerprints. Infrared photography has many applications, however the most important is its ability to resolve objects at greater distances

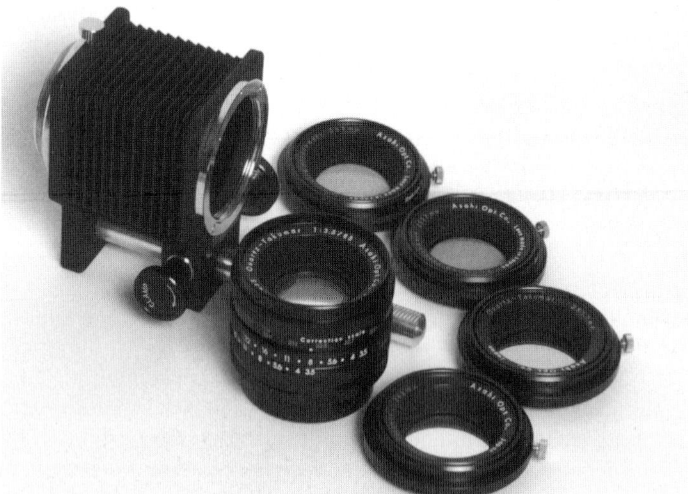

The Quartz-Takumar 85mm f/3.5 was the first lens Pentax introduced for use in ultraviolet light. It came with two sets of filters and a bellows attachment. As it is a short-mount lens, the bellows acts as its focusing mechanism.

than conventional photography allows. The military uses it to detect camouflage.

Conventional lenses contain glass elements, which block out most UV wavelengths. The 85mm lenses are made with fluorite and quartz elements; the quartz elements allow these lenses to transmit UV wavelengths. When taking visible spectrum photographs with quartz-element lenses, a UV filter must be used. Without this accessory, the image is rendered flat, lacking contrast, or it may appear to be fogged. The Quartz-Takumar 85mm f/3.5 lens can be used for UV and conventional photography, and the Ultra-Achromatic Takumar 85mm f/4.5 can be used for infrared and UV photography, as well as conventional photography (with a UV filter). The 300mm f/5.6 lens is made with glass and fluorite elements, allowing it to produce excellent photographs in both the visible and infrared portions of the spectrum.

The Quartz-Takumar 85mm f/3.5 lens requires "viewing" and "taking" filters, because ultra-violet and visible light come to sharp focus at different points. The lens is supplied with two sets of viewing and taking filters, one for 253.7mμ and the other for 365mμ, which enable you to take photographs at two different ultraviolet wavelengths. In practice, the photographer focuses with the filter-like focusing attachment in place, then carefully replaces that filter with the corresponding taking filter. Filters must be exchanged without introducing any movement, so a tripod is recommended.

The Ultra-Achromatic Takumar 85mm f/4.5 lens came with three filters for infrared shooting, the R62, R68, and 862mμ; and one for UV photography, the 365mμ. Unlike its predecessor, it

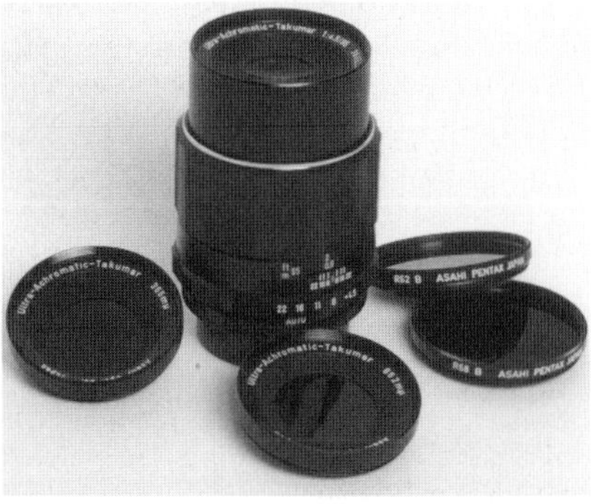

The Ultra-Achromatic Takumar 85mm f/4.5 lens was sold with four filters that are used to correct for infrared and ultraviolet wavelengths.

can be used for both infrared and ultraviolet photography, and no focus-shift manipulation is necessary. To take a photograph, first focus conventionally, and then attach the appropriate filter to the lens. When the filter is screwed onto the front of the lens, the front element is pushed back into the lens housing, creating the proper focus compensation.

As mentioned, the Ultra-Achromatic Takumar 300mm f/5.6 lens is a high-resolution lens that can be used to shoot both infrared and visible light. It was not sold with filters, as the others were, but any 58mm filter can be used with this lens. Infrared focus compensation is performed by focusing in the conventional way. Because the lens is fully corrected in the infrared region, no focus compensation is necessary.

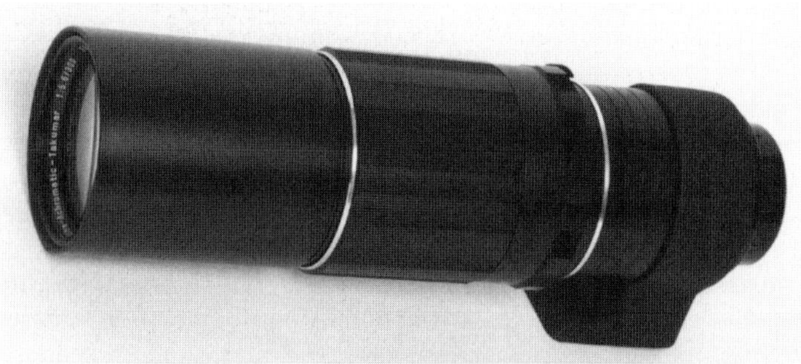

The Ultra-Achromatic Takumar 300mm f/5.6 can be used to photograph subjects in both infrared and visible light.

Super Multi-Coated (SMC) Takumar Lenses

Often abbreviated SMC Takumar, Super Multi-Coated Takumar lenses were introduced in 1971 with the Spotmatic II camera. They were equipped with a feature that Asahi pioneered: multiple lens coatings that reduced internal flare—a design that caused sweeping changes within the industry.

Even though earlier Pentax lenses contained so-called "automatic" diaphragms, they needed to be stopped down in order for exposure to be determined. (Some Spotmatic models contained a light meter switch, while some Takumar lenses possessed a depth-of-field preview lever. A light meter switch turns the meter on and stops the lens down; a depth-of-field lever stops the lens down, but does not activate the light meter.) Most SMC Takumar lenses allowed meter readings to be taken with the lens at full aperture.

Meter readings on a Spotmatic F can be made with a wide-open aperture using most SMC Takumar lenses. However, if you want to use earlier, non-automatic lenses, you can use stopped-down metering.

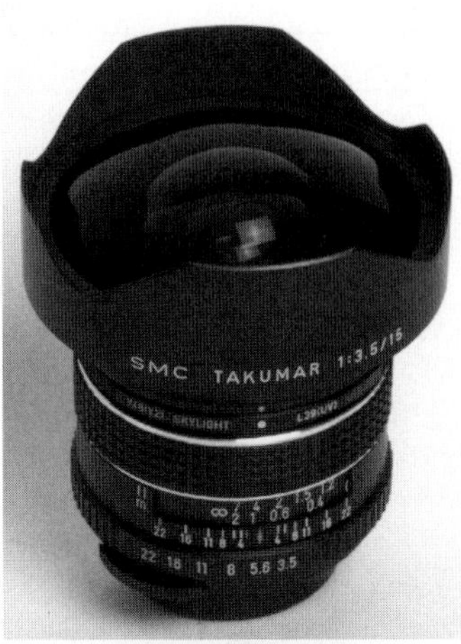

SMC Takumar 15mm f/3.5

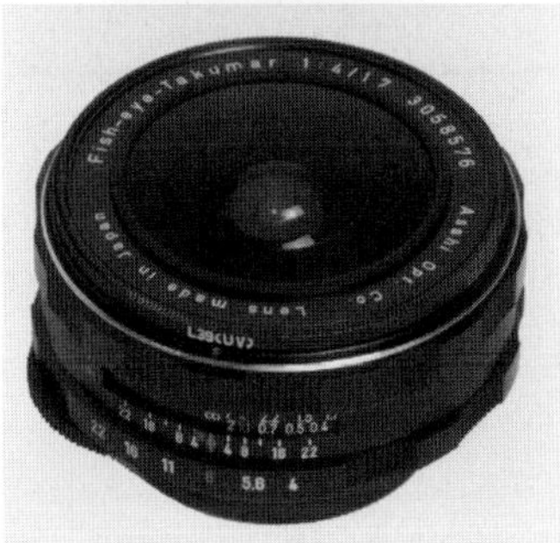

SMC Takumar Fisheye 17mm f/4

Asahi Bayonet-Mount Lenses

As photography became more sophisticated, Asahi realized they could not offer adequate lens-to-camera data transfer unless they abandoned their screw-mount lens system. Every camera manufacturer eventually made some lens-data transfer modifications. Many photographers were unhappy with this change, but eventually, even the most skeptical became convinced that progress demands change.

In 1975 Asahi stopped production on its screw-mount lenses. At that time they also stopped using the name "Takumar." Since 1957, every camera manufactured by Asahi had borne the name Pentax. It was good marketing strategy to use one name for all their products. Therefore, the new bayonet-mount (or K-mount) lenses were called "SMC Pentax" lenses. They were compatible with the new Pentax K cameras introduced that same year.

More than a decade later, Asahi reintroduced the Takumar name; it was used to designate some special-market lenses. But during the "K-mount years," the name Takumar referred to screw-mount lenses.

SMC Pentax Lenses

When the new Pentax K-mount lenses appeared on the market in 1975, most of them were identical to their screw-mount counterparts with only the mount being changed. In other cases, the minimum aperture was reduced or the filter size was changed.

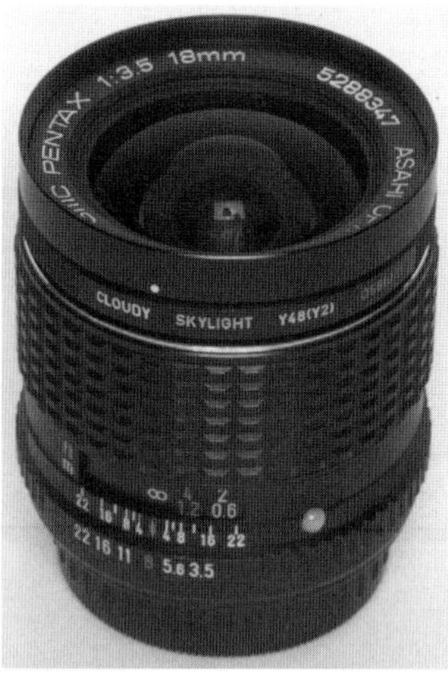

SMC Pentax 18mm f/3.5

As time went on, new lenses were added to the SMC lineup. Lenses with unusual focal lengths, larger apertures, and some zoom lenses rounded out the original Pentax bayonet lens family.

Owners of Asahi screw-mount lenses can use them on bayonet-mount Pentax bodies thanks to the Pentax screw-to-bayonet lens adapter, Mount Adapter K. It allows screw-mount lenses to focus to infinity when used on a bayonet-mount camera, while most lens adapters do not. This adapter does not allow for automatic diaphragm or normal light meter functions. See page 182.

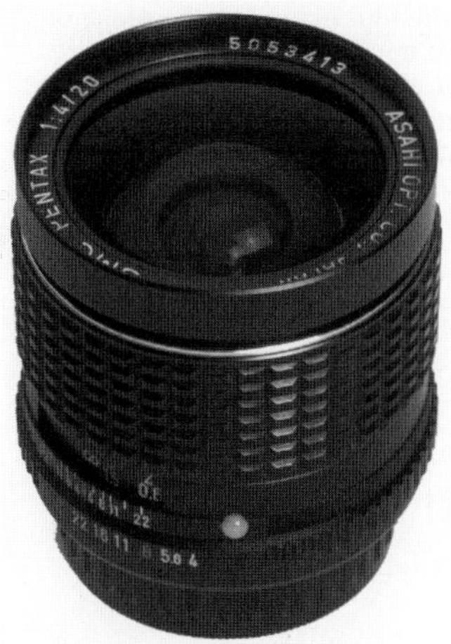

SMC Pentax 20mm f/4

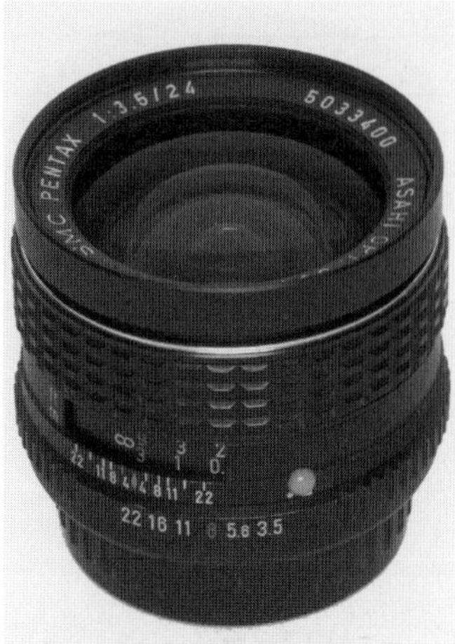

SMC Pentax 24mm f/3.5

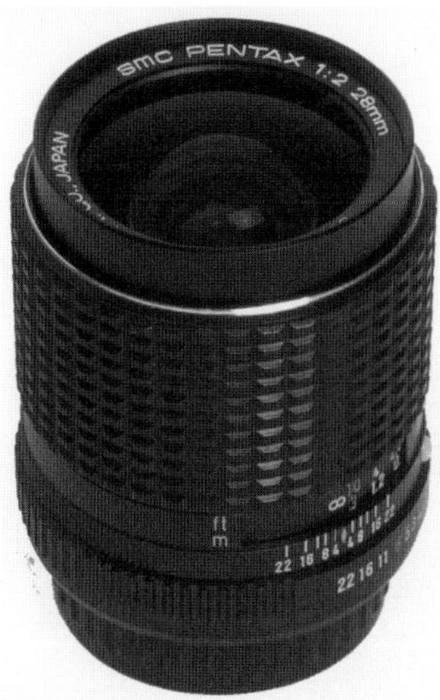

SMC Pentax 28mm f/2

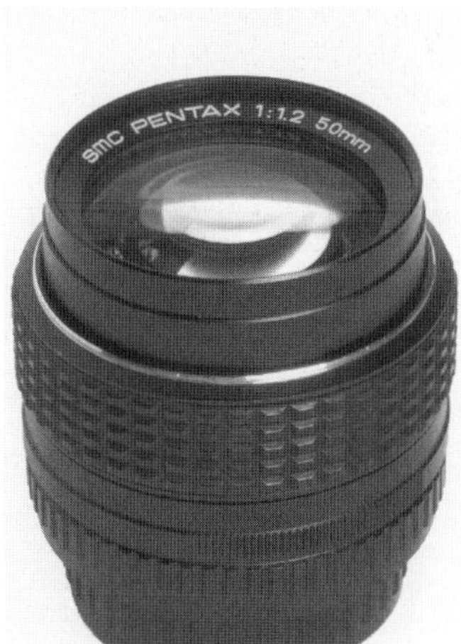

SMC Pentax 50mm f/1.2

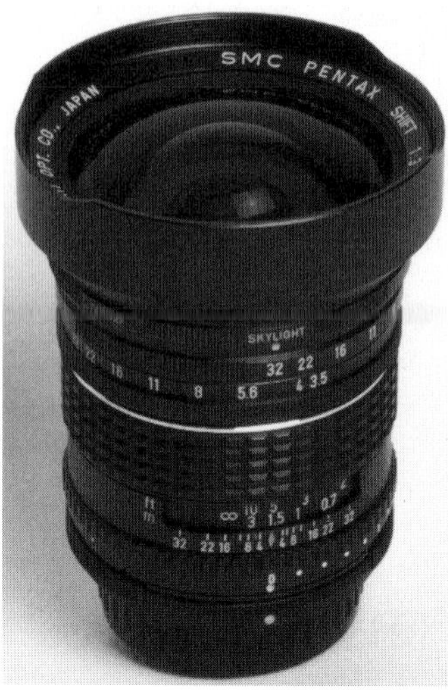

If the film plane and the plane of a subject, such as a building, are not parallel, the subject's straight lines will appear to converge. The SMC Pentax 28mm f/3.5 Shift lens can help eliminate or exaggerate this effect.

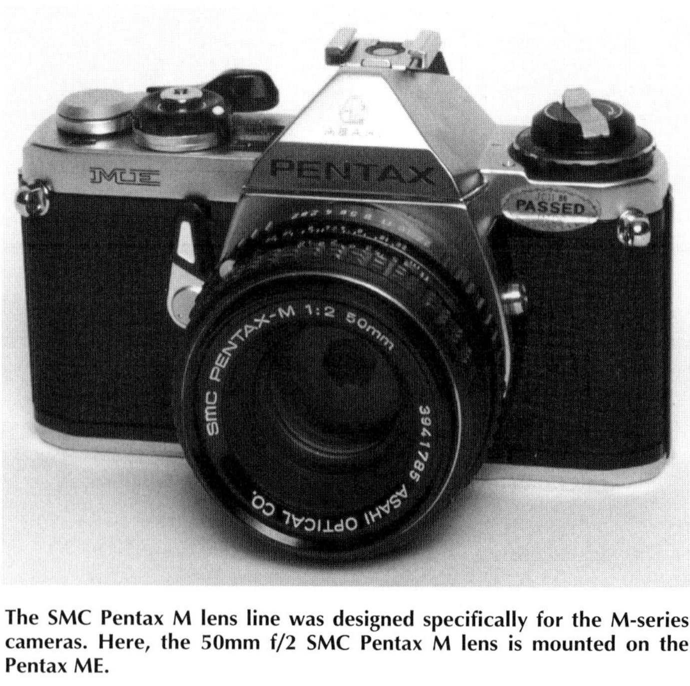

The SMC Pentax M lens line was designed specifically for the M-series cameras. Here, the 50mm f/2 SMC Pentax M lens is mounted on the Pentax ME.

SMC Pentax M Lenses

In the seventies there was a trend to make more lightweight, compact cameras, and in response, Asahi redesigned their camera line with the Pentax ME and MX. For these small-sized SLRs, Asahi carefully redesigned smaller, lighter lenses—called SMC Pentax M lenses. In many cases, these lenses were replacements for their older, larger counterparts. Sometimes the lens speed or the minimum focusing distance would change. Eventually, new lenses were introduced to the "M" line that had not appeared in earlier lens series.

As a new "M" lens was introduced, the older "SMC" version would disappear from Asahi's catalog pages. Since the lenses' functions were identical in both series, "M" lenses are compatible with all the older bayonet-mount 35mm Pentax cameras and vice versa.

The most compact "M" lens offered was the 40mm f/2.8 SMC Pentax M. When mounted to a body, it adds only 18mm to the camera's overall size. This lens mounted on any compact Pentax makes an extremely tiny, very versatile package that rivals many point-and-shoots for size, but exceeds their versatility in countless ways. This 40mm "M" lens has become highly collectible. Aficionados pay premium prices for mint-condition specimens.

SMC Pentax A Lenses

By 1983, when cameras came out with a fully automatic Program mode, Asahi entered the race to solve the final design issue in the automation of non-autofocus cameras. Program mode requires that the camera's electronics be able to set both shutter speed and aperture. To accomplish this, Pentax lenses had to be redesigned so that electrical contacts in the lens and body could channel communication that allows the lens' iris diaphragm to execute commands originating in the camera's computer center. Asahi called these lenses "SMC Pentax A" lenses, and they were introduced with the Pentax Super A camera. This new A-series lens system functioned equally well with K-mount Pentax cameras. All the advanced functions of earlier SMC lenses, such as full-aperture viewing, were retained. This allowed Asahi to eventually discontinue most of the K-series lenses. As before, the early A lenses were almost identical to their earlier counterparts, and again, the A lens series expanded with the passage of time.

SMC Pentax F Lenses

When Asahi introduced its new line of autofocus 35mm SLR cameras, it was again necessary to alter the lens lineup. Built around the popular K mount and introduced in 1987 with the SF series of autofocus cameras, the new SMC Pentax F lenses are compatible with both non-autofocus and autofocus cameras. The older, non-autofocus lenses are still compatible with new autofocus cameras. Of course, a manual focus lens on an autofocus body will not focus automatically; conversely, an autofocus lens on a manual focus body will not focus automatically. Automation, in any system, is always limited by its least automatic component. (Only one autofocus lens was available for the MEF, however it was *not* an F lens. See page 109 for more information.)

SMC Pentax FA Lenses

This lens line was introduced with the Pentax PZ series of cameras in 1991. SMC Pentax FA lenses are similar in function to SMC Pentax F lenses, but contain two additional features that are not usable on the Pentax cameras covered in this book—power zoom and a microchip for use with cameras that offer MTF (Modular Transfer Function) Priority Program mode.

Flash Photography

Basic Flash Principles

Most modern flash units allow anyone to take flash pictures without having to make time-consuming computations. Nevertheless, when using flash for creative photography, most photographers find that it is still beneficial to understand how flash works. Here are some flash fundamentals.

Light Output, Duration, and Distance

In flash photography, exposure is determined by many things, including the amount of light output by the flash unit, the duration of the light, the distance between the subject and the flash unit, and the aperture. The subject will receive less light the farther it is located from the source of the light. Light from a flash unit is subject to the Inverse Square Law, which states that *the amount of light decreases in proportion to the square of the distance it travels.*

Thus, doubling the light increases the shooting range only by slightly less than 1-1/2 times. Therefore, if the flash provides correct exposure for a subject 10 feet (3 meters) away with the camera lens set at an aperture of f/5.6, opening the lens 1 full stop to f/4 will provide correct exposure only as far as 14 feet (4.3 meters), not 20 feet (6 meters). Opening the aperture 1 stop allows twice as much light to pass, but the flash will reach only 1.4 times as far. Again, this is determined by the Inverse Square Law.

Guide Numbers

A guide number (GN) quantifies the relationship between brightness, distance, and film sensitivity and assists in calculating aperture and distance values in practical applications. Guide numbers are usually stated using ISO 100 film as the standard. While these calculations are generally unnecessary with today's automatic flash equipment, they sometimes are used in situations where manual adjustments to the flash output are required. Even when using a camera with Through-the-Lens (TTL) flash metering, flash exposure compensation may occasionally be necessary.

Guide numbers follow a logarithmic progression comparable to f/stops. A numerically larger guide number means more light, while a numerically larger f/stop means less light. For example, if the distance from the subject and the guide number corresponding to the film sensitivity are known, the aperture required to obtain the correct exposure for a subject at a given distance can be easily determined.

Aperture = Guide Number/Distance

Note: In the United States, guide numbers are expressed in feet, and are consequently 3.3 times larger than corresponding metric guide numbers. When making this calculation, make sure that the guide number and distance are expressed in the same unit of measurement.

Guide Numbers with Zoom Flash Heads

Typically, guide numbers are based on the image angle of a standard 50mm lens. However, the guide number will change if the flash unit's angle of illumination is changed. With zoom flash heads, the angle of illumination is modified to cover the angle of view of different lenses. This is often accomplished by changing the position of the flash-head diffuser, or the reflector, in relation to the flash tube. By adjusting the zoom head, the flash energy is either concentrated on a smaller angle of illumination, which covers a longer distance, or diffused over a larger angle, which covers a shorter distance. The smaller the angle of illumination (long focal length lenses), the greater the guide number; the greater the angle of illumination (short focal length lenses), the smaller the guide number.

This explains why a flash unit—even though it always emits the same quantity of light—will have several different guide numbers when the zoom head is adjusted to cover various angles.

Color Temperature

The light from most flash units has a color temperature of 5600° Kelvin (5600° K), which approximates daylight. Because of this, flash is an excellent source of light for augmenting natural light in fill-flash photography. Daylight-balanced film (rather than tungsten) should be used for flash photography.

Red-Eye

Red-eye occurs most often when using an on-camera flash unit because the flash axis and lens axis are almost the same. When this occurs, the light from the flash reflects off the eye's retina and back into the lens, onto the film. When there is a significant distance between the lens and flash axis however, this red light is reflected out of the image area. Diffusing or bouncing the light from the flash helps reduce red-eye, but it also reduces the flash intensity. A better alternative is to use a flash bracket, such as those manufactured by Stroboframe. These brackets raise the flash high above the camera, away from the lens axis, effectively eliminating red-eye.

Flash Synchronization

For proper results, the electronic flash must fire when the focal plane shutter is completely open. The shutter consists of two curtains that move in sequence across the film. The first curtain opens, uncovers the film for exposure, and then the second curtain closes, providing a light-tight cover over the film again. Exposure time is changed by releasing the second curtain either sooner or later. Thus, the fastest synchronization speed for electronic flash is the fastest shutter speed at which the first curtain has completely uncovered the film and the second has not yet begun to close. Some SLRs have vertically traveling metal blades, which synchronize at a much higher speed. The principle of operation is much the same as the older, horizontally traveling shutters. Remember, the synchronization speed only indicates the fastest possible shutter speed for a flash exposure. Slower speeds can be used.

The fastest shutter sync speed is usually indicated on the camera. Some have the speed marked in red, others have an X next to the speed (or just an X without a speed), and some have the X and are marked in red.

If the focal plane shutter is set at a speed faster than the fastest synchronization speed, only a portion of the image area will be exposed. The remainder of the film area, which was still covered by a curtain during the flash burst, will be severely underexposed or black. Some cameras, including the ME Super, MV, MV-1, MG, and MEF, automatically prevent this error. They simply refuse to fire a flash at too fast a speed, and automatically default to the fastest possible synchronization speed. These "smart" cameras will protect against improper shutter speed settings only if they

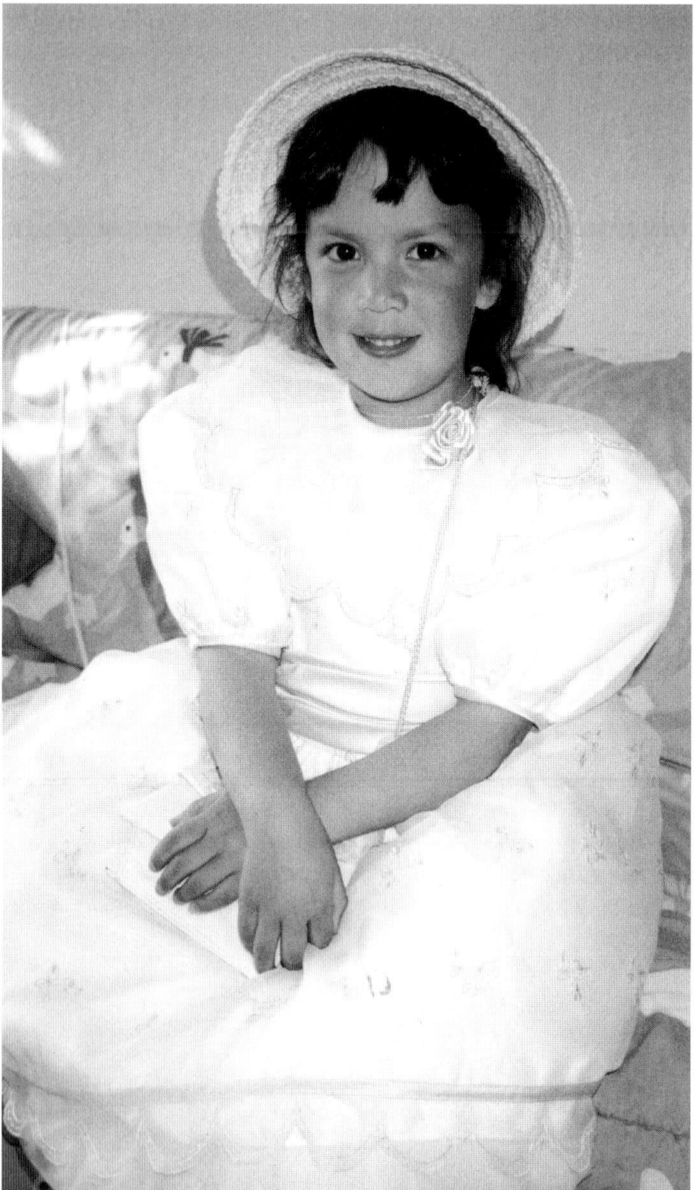

are being used with a dedicated flash *and* both camera and flash are set in Automatic mode.

Autoflash Modes

In order to understand the advantages and limitations of different autoflash modes, the photographer should have a basic knowledge of how they operate.

Conventional Automatic Flash

Early automatic flash units base their exposure on a photoelectric sensor, found on the front of the flash unit, which reads the light reflected from the subject. When this sensor determines that exposure is adequate, the flash switches off. This type of automation results in fairly well-exposed images within a certain distance range and under normal conditions. Unlike more advanced TTL automation, sensor flash does not compensate for the angle of view of different lens focal lengths, ambient lighting conditions, or the use of filters. Even so, when this type of automation was introduced, automatic sensor flash units were regarded as a giant step forward. Some of today's aftermarket flash units still are made on this principle.

TTL Flash Automation

Unlike with sensor autoflash, with TTL autoflash the light from the exposure is calculated after it passes through the lens. The mirror flips up, the aperture closes down, the shutter curtain opens fully, and then the flash fires. While the shutter is open, a flash metering cell usually found in the lower portion of the mirror chamber measures the light reflected off the film. Based on this measurement, the camera's electronics turn off the flash at the appropriate time.

When family comes calling, make sure your camera and flash are ready; rapidly growing loved ones should be recorded at every stage of their lives. Electronic flash is the ideal light source for moments like this. If your subject is patient, try several different lighting treatments: direct flash, bounce flash, and possibly a flash-window light combination. But take care...subjects often get bored before you exhaust your ideas!

The Pentax AF280T flash unit features TTL flash control and head that will bounce, tilt down to –15°, and swivel. A flash head that tilts down below the horizontal position is essential for macro photography.

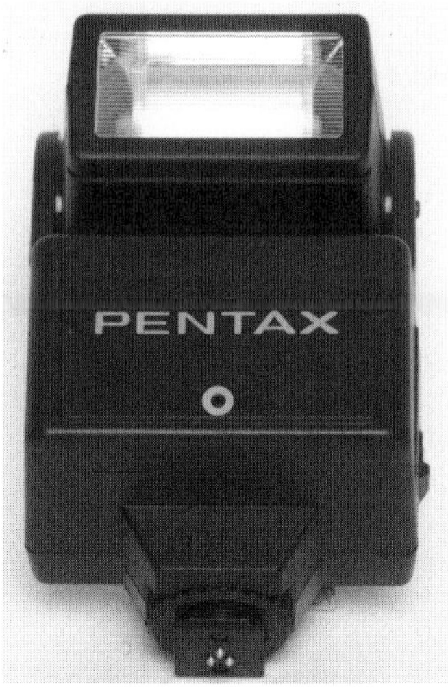

Compared with sensor autoflash units, TTL flash measures the exposure throughout the lens' angle of view. Lens attachments or filters are thus also taken into consideration. In TTL flash mode, the aperture set on the lens is of relatively little consequence to the flash exposure because different apertures are automatically compensated for by the flash unit.

Limitations of TTL Flash

There are limitations to this system. For instance, when the main subject does not fill the frame and the background is quite a distance away, only a fraction of the light emitted by the flash is reflected by the subject. The remainder of this light is lost in the background. The TTL autoflash attempts to counteract this by prolonging the duration of the flash. The result is often an overexposed main subject, especially if it is in the foreground.

If a subject absorbs or reflects light in an unusual manner, the TTL flash exposure may not be ideal. The TTL adjustment "assumes" that the subject has average reflecting power or is "medium gray." Naturally dark subjects, with low reflectance, will be overly lit. Conversely, very light subjects with high reflectance will be underlit, appearing too dark in the final photo. A bride dressed in white in front of a white wall will be rendered too dark; a black cat in front of a black wall will be rendered too light. If you want to improve on this, you can set the flash and the camera to Manual flash mode or use the flash unit's exposure compensation setting.

The Test Flash Feature

Most flash units allow you to fire a test flash without exposing the film by triggering it manually. Actually, this button allows you to conduct two tests. The first one proves the flash unit's ability to fire (but not the camera's). If the camera and flash are in the Automatic mode, you can also test for proper flash-to-subject distance. However, a test flash burst is not appraised by the TTL metering system in the camera; it is only read by the sensor built into the flash unit. If the test indicator has a positive response, the flash output will probably be sufficient for correct exposure.

Flash Terminology and Specific Pentax Cameras

When considering flash capability, the Pentax cameras detailed in this book fall into three categories—no camera-derived flash automation, dedicated flash, and Through-the-Lens (TTL) capabilities.

The cameras without automatic flash mechanisms can synchronize with electronic flash units, but must be set manually or rely on the flash unit's sensor automation. The Pentax cameras covered in this book with no flash automation include all the Spotmatics, the K2, KM, KX, ME, and MX.

To have dedicated flash and camera operation, the camera and flash must be compatible. With Pentax cameras, flash dedication means that the shutter speed is set automatically to the X sync speed by the camera's electronic system, although the camera's f/stop must be set manually to the aperture recommended by the flash unit's dial or chart. This dedicated setting of the sync speed occurs only when the shutter speed dial is set to AUTO. If desired, the photographer can override this automation (thereby losing dedication) by setting the shutter speed dial manually to select a slower shutter speed. Cameras with dedicated flash capability generally feature a flash ready light in the viewfinder, which signals that the flash is fully charged and ready to fire. The Pentax cameras covered in this book that have flash dedication are the ME Super, MEF, MG, MV, and MV-1.

With TTL flash automation the camera is capable of setting everything, assuring excellent flash exposures every time under normal conditions. However the photographer must take care that the flash-lens combination is capable of delivering enough light to cover the required flash-to-subject distance. Naturally, the photographer must also select an f/stop that will permit adequate light transmission to the film. The Pentax LX is the only camera covered in this book that offers TTL flash metering.

Note: A camera featuring flash automation is capable of any or all of the less automated flash functions. For example, a camera with TTL flash metering is also dedicated and can be used in the Automatic or Manual flash modes, but a non-dedicated flash unit cannot perform TTL flash metering.

Pentax Electronic Flash Units

Over the years, Pentax has offered many electronic flash units for sale. It would require more than one volume to cover all the features of the numerous flashes and how each flash unit interfaces with the different cameras. Some of the electronic flash units offered by Pentax over the classic period include the Super-Lite Electronic Flash, AF-16, AF-160, AF-200S, AF-280T, AF-400T, and the AF-080C Ring Light. These flash units span the spectrum. The Super-Lite is by today's standards a very elementary unit; the TTL units, such as the AF-400T and the AF-080C, are state-of-the-art units. And the Pentax LX is timeless—flash units made when it was new have been replaced by units that function with autofocus cameras. The LX is completely at home with all these flash units, new and old. Owning a Pentax camera is comforting; the Asahi Optical Company has exhibited fierce loyalty to their customer base. Intentional obsolescence has never been their policy.

It is easy to determine the compatibility of a camera-flash combination; simply look at the camera's accessory shoe and the flash unit's foot. If they both have the same number of electrical contact points and those points mate, the set is a match. If either contains more contact points than the other, the unit with fewer contact points will be the limiting factor. For example, a flash

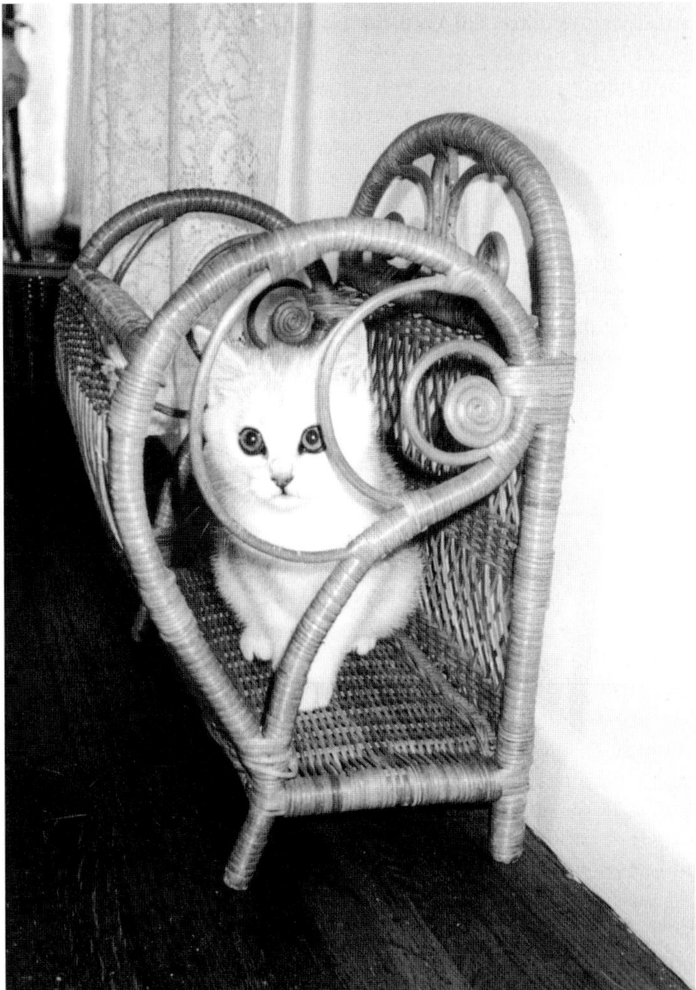

Flash photography is the easy way to capture priceless, fleeting indoor moments. Direct flash would have created harsh light and shadows. Bounce flash produced a softer effect. If your electronic flash has bounce capability, use it whenever possible.

unit that contains TTL flash metering cannot magically make a non-TTL flash metering camera function in that mode.

If a flash unit makes contact through the PC terminal, it will, by definition, be an automatic or a manual flash (TTL flash metering is not possible without more electrical contact points than a PC terminal allows). If a camera's hot shoe contains only one contact point, plus the ground, it cannot transfer TTL flash metering data.

However, virtually every electronic flash with a standard foot will function with any Pentax camera. Conversely, every camera included in this book will function with most electronic flash units. Incompatibility can occur in varying degrees, but usually not completely. If any question arises, help is as close as your nearest camera store. As a general rule, when shopping for flash units and accessories for the cameras covered in this book, it is best to buy from a specialty photographic retailer who knows and understands older SLR equipment.

Flash Bulbs

Before electronic flash became popular and affordable, flash bulbs were commonly used. In 1960, when the Spot-Matic was announced, virtually no one used electronic flash. By the time the Spotmatic line was discontinued, flash bulbs were all but extinct. Some of the cameras covered in this book were designed for use with both electronic flash and flash bulbs. Though somewhat academic, flash bulb information is discussed below.

Over the years flash bulbs have been offered in many sizes and varieties. Early flash bulbs were large. They had a base commonly called a "medium screw base"—the same base as a standard household light bulb. And some of the glass envelopes were quite large, resembling 250-watt light bulbs. Some examples of this bulb type include the number 11, the number 22, the number 31, and the Press 40. As films became faster, smaller flash bulbs were developed.

Flash bulbs were also manufactured to synchronize with specific types of shutter designs—bulbs designed to be used with between-the-lens (leaf) shutters burn at a different rate than focal plane (FP) bulbs. Between-the-lens (leaf) shutters expose the entire frame of film at the same instant. Focal plane shutters of early design expose the film via a narrow slit that exposes the film in segments (focal plane shutters are said to "wipe the image onto the film"). Therefore, flash bulbs were made to accommodate these two different types of shutters: short-duration bulbs and flat-peak bulbs. Flash bulbs fall into three categories that designate their combustion rate. Medium-peak (M) and fast-peak (F) bulbs (classified as short-duration bulbs), and focal plane bulbs (classified as flat-peak bulbs).

The next evolution of the flash bulb brought the "S.C. Bayonet Base" into vogue. S.C. is the abbreviation for "Single Contact." Most of these bulbs have a glass envelope approximately the size of a standard spool of thread. Some examples of this bulb type include the SM, the number 5, the number 25, the number 6, and the number 26.

Flash bulb sizes and bases got smaller and smaller (M2 and M5) until there was no base left; just two wires (contacts) protruded from the envelope (the AG1). This AG1 bulb appeared in flash cubes (consisting of four AG1s mounted together in a rotatable base), flash bars (multiple AG1s mounted horizontally in a plastic housing), and "flip flash" configurations. These multiply housed bulbs made flash-bulb photography easier and faster, but nothing could stop the electronic flash avalanche.

Flash bulbs were originally designed for use with black-and-white film. Clear bulbs were not compatible with daylight-balanced color films. Blue filters could be used over the camera lens, blue flash shields were used to cover flash bulbs (flash bulbs did occasionally explode, sometimes with disastrous results), and there were even films sold that were balanced for use with clear flash bulbs (type F film). The most common solution for daylight-balanced color film and flash photography was the blue flash bulb. A blue bulb was identified by the letter "B" in its title: AG1B, M5B, Press 40B, and so on.

Early flash units were usually attached to the tripod socket and were powered by size D batteries. They were a large addition to the gadget bag. As bulbs got smaller, so did the flash units. As bulb bases changed, the receptacles in the flash units changed as well. Adapters were sold so that smaller bulbs could be used in larger flash units.

Aside from the bulb sizes there were differences in their characteristics. Some bulbs were gas-filled, early ones were foil-filled, but most were wire-filled. The material that filled the envelope was less important to the user than the burn rate of the bulb. When a flash bulb is fired it takes some time to reach its peak intensity. Manufacturers of the shutters used in cameras and photographic lenses synchronized the time that the shutter opens to correspond with the time of the flash bulb's maximum light output.

Instructions for precise synchronization and operation of each type of flash bulb are located on every box of bulbs. Also included is a chart that indicates how the enclosed bulbs sync with every shutter type, and at which shutter speeds sync occurs. Another chart details exposure information on the flash bulb box. If the photographer does not know which type of bulb is best, a comparison of the data on several types of flash bulb boxes should settle all doubts.

Pentax Classic Accessories

Over the years, there have been many accessories manufactured for Pentax cameras, some by the Asahi Optical Company, others subcontracted for them, and some by aftermarket sources. One entire volume could not cover every item manufactured that will function on or with a Pentax camera. We will concern ourselves here with the major accessories that bear the Asahi and/or Pentax name and are usable with the cameras covered in this book. Not every accessory will function with every model, and those distinctions will be noted.

Lens Accessories

The most common accessory for any camera outfit is a filter. Even the person who does not use filters to alter their images probably owns at least one haze-reducing, lens-protecting filter.

Filters

The Asahi Optical Company has an extensive line of filters in sizes that fit their lenses. Companies, such as Tiffen, which manufacture filters as one of their primary product lines, must provide filters to fit virtually any lens ever sold. Camera manufacturers usually supply only filters that are sized to fit their lenses, and sometimes only for the more popular sizes. At the time that most of the cameras described in this book were in vogue, Asahi was supplying lens accessories in the following sizes: 49mm, 52mm, 58mm, 67mm, and 77mm. Some accessories, like the gelatin filter holder, were supplied only in 49mm, 52mm, 58mm, and 77mm.

We will not cover the use of filters in this chapter, but will enumerate the Asahi filters available to the Pentax camera owners of this era. There are many excellent books that describe the use of filters. The Kodak Workshop Series book *Using Filters* is ideal and can be obtained at most any well-stocked camera shop or book store.

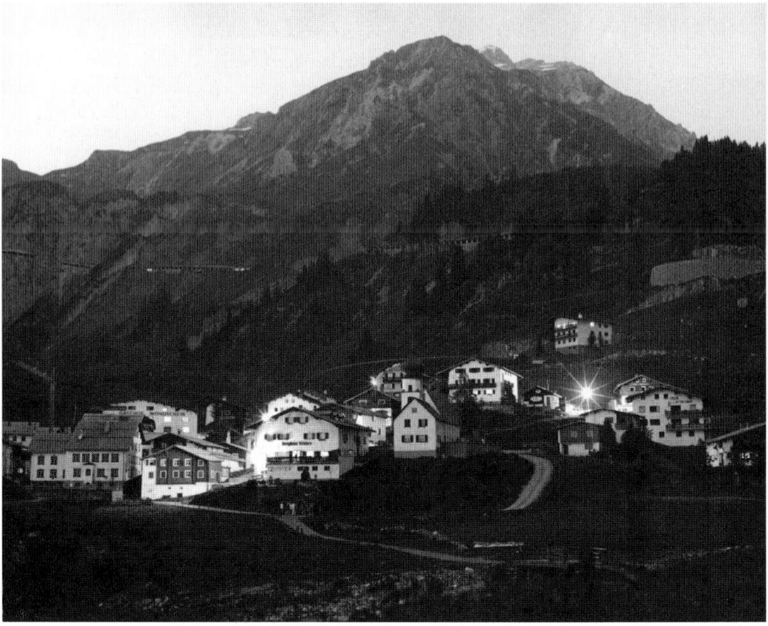

The right filter can change the entire tone of a photo. When a star filter is used, it should not be overbearing, but simply add a subtle touch of interest to the scene.

Black-and-white filters: The principal filters for shooting with black-and-white film are UV (ultraviolet), Y1 (light yellow), Y2 (medium yellow), O2 (orange), R2 (red), and YG (yellow-green).

Color filters: Asahi filters' names often describe their use. For color film, Asahi offered Skylight, Cloudy (equivalent to a Wratten 81A), Morning and Evening (cooling filters), Flash (for use with clear flashbulbs and daylight color film), Photoflood (for daylight color film and clear photofloods), and Fluorescent (for shooting with daylight color films under fluorescent lights). Asahi makes current models of most of these filters.

A polarizing filter can be used with black-and-white or color films. Asahi made both linear and circular polarizing filters. Most cameras mentioned in this book will function with either, but the autofocus system of the Pentax MEF and the light metering system

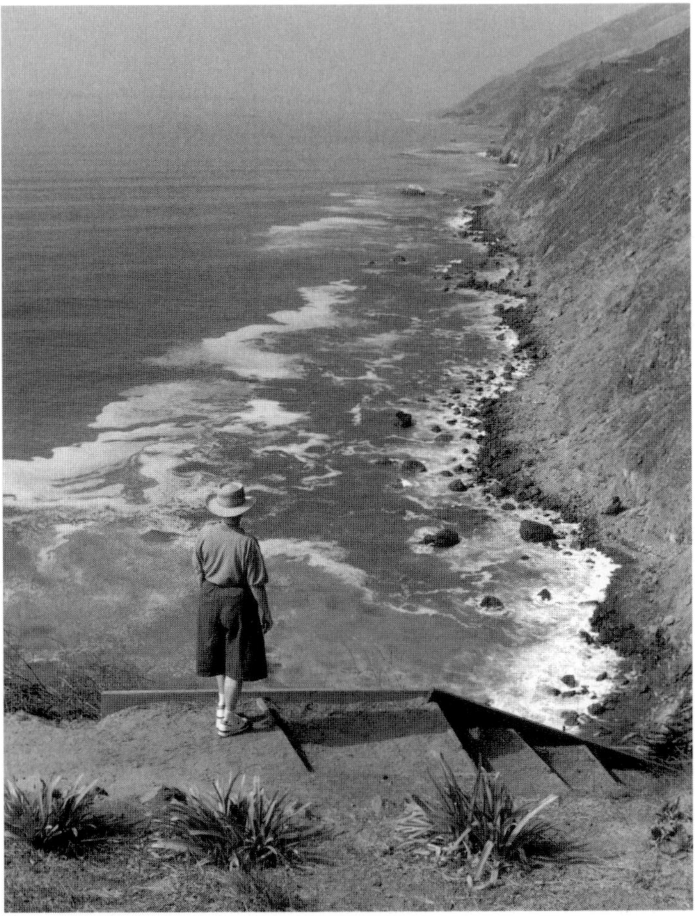

This image was created on a hazy day. A medium yellow (Y2) filter was used to reproduce the scene as the eye saw it.

of the Pentax LX require a circular polarizing filter. (Asahi currently makes only circular polarizers, as they are what their current line of cameras requires.)

Special Filter Series: Also offered for sale during this era were lens attachments called the "Special Filter Series"; some were for use

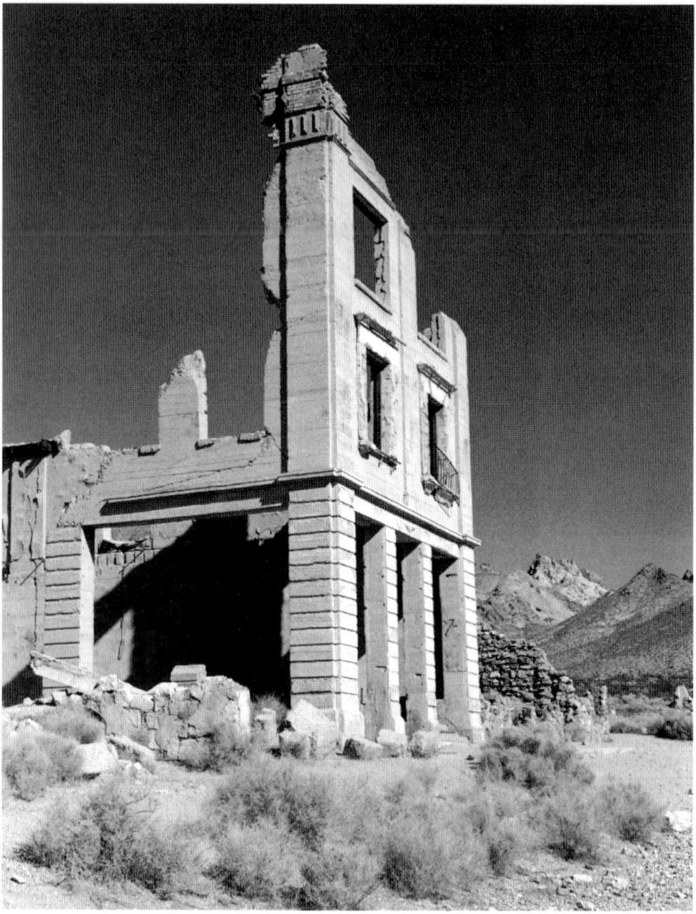

This ghost town contains so many strong images, every photographer who visits it leaves with lots of exposed film. A red (R2) filter was used to darken the sky and increase the contrast in this image.

with color films, others for use with both monochromatic and color films. The Special Filter Series was available in 49mm and 52mm filter sizes. It included the Fantastic Color filters, Magic Image Attachments, and a Fluorescent Light filter that corrects for fluorescent light when using daylight color film.

The Fantastic Color Filter R/B changes from red to blue when the filter ring is rotated. Intermediate hues can be achieved and the effect observed in the viewfinder. The Fantastic Color Filter R/G varies the color from red to amber and then to green as its ring is rotated.

Asahi offered five Magic Image Attachments that screw onto the lens like a filter. The Magic Image Attachment 5C has five facets plus a flat center, creating six images of the featured subject. The Magic Image Attachment 4C produces five images of the subject, and the Magic Image Attachment 2C yields one dominant and two fainter images of the central subject. The Magic Image Attachment 6M has five parallel facets on one half of its surface with a plain second half, producing six images of the subject. The Magic Image Attachment CF is essentially a soft-focus filter that is sharp in the center.

SMC filters: Asahi was a pioneer in the field of placing "Super Multi-Coatings" on optical surfaces. As the name implies, many separate layers (up to seven) of coating are applied to the surface of the filter. These layers of coating reduce reflections as no single layer can. During this era, Asahi offered SMC filters for sale in the following combinations:

49mm = UV, Y2, O2, R2, Skylight, and Cloudy
52mm = UV, Y2, O2, R2, Skylight, and Cloudy
58mm = UV, Y2, O2, and Skylight
67mm = UV, Y2, O2, and Skylight
77mm = UV, Y2, O2, and Skylight

Gelatin Filter Holder

The Pentax Gelatin Filter Holder holds gelatin filters that are 3 inches square. The accessory filter frame is used in conjunction with the holder to house gelatin filters. This gelatin filter holder was offered in four sizes: 49mm, 52mm, 58mm, and 77mm. Asahi has since added one more size to their line, 67mm.

Close-up Lenses

Pentax offers close-up lenses that screw onto the front of the lens like a filter. Although these are lens attachments, they are also close-up accessories. They are explained in more detail on page 160.

Lens Hoods

Pentax made, and continues to make, lens hoods for their lenses. Hood styles include rectangular, round, rubber, and specialty hoods. Because Asahi/Takumar/Pentax lenses have continued to use the same lens diameters over the years, lens hoods sold today usually work fine on older lenses. A 50mm focal length lens that requires a 49mm (filter diameter) hood will function properly with a 49mm hood of any vintage. However, it is best if you use a lens and hood from the same era or series for greatest compatibility. You may want to run a test to see if the hood vignettes before using it at an important event.

Close-up Accessories

All camera-lens combinations have limitations as to how close they can focus on a subject. If a photographer wants to focus closer than the camera-lens combination will allow, a close-up accessory or close-focusing device is required. These include close-up lenses, extension tubes, bellows, and macro lenses.

Close-up Lenses

Pentax produced a wider variety of close-up lenses in the past than they do today. Pentax close-up lenses and their applications are shown below.

Close-up Lens	SMC Pentax Lens	Lens-to-Subject Distance Range*	Magnification Range*
S25	40mm f/2.8 50mm f/1.4 50mm f/1.7 50mm f/2 55mm f/1.8 55mm f/2	32.6–22.0cm	1:4.8–1:2.7
S40	40mm f/2.8 50mm f/1.4 50mm f/1.7 50mm f/2 55mm f/1.8 55mm f/2	48.0–27.0cm	1:7.6–1:3.5

Close-up Lens	SMC Pentax Lens	Lens-to-Subject Distance Range*	Magnification Range*
T80	85 to 150mm	91.6–50.5cm (with 85mm f/2)	1:9.4–1:4.2 (with 85mm f/2)
T95	135mm f/2.5 200mm f/4	114.0–84.0cm	1:4.8–1:2.6
T160	100 to 150mm	175.0–89.5cm (with 135mm f/3.5)	1:11.9–1:4.9 (with 135mm f/3.5)
T183	135mm f/2.5 200mm f/4	202.0–113.0cm	1:9.1–1:3.8

**The Lens-to-Subject Distance and Magnification ranges listed are true for the specific lens cited. The values can be applied only as approximations for the other lenses listed within each Close-up Lens category.*

Extension Tubes

When a lens is focused at infinity, it is at its most compact configuration. The closer the lens is focused, the farther the lens elements move away from the camera body. When the lens' internal helical focusing track has been extended to its maximum distance, the lens is set at its minimum focusing distance. Extension tubes mount between the camera body and the lens, extending the distance from the lens elements to the film plane, thus allowing the lens to focus at closer distances. Extension tubes do not contain any lens elements; they are simply light-tight, empty tubes that serve only to increase the distance of the lens to the camera body.

Pentax and other suppliers offer extension tubes for screw-mount and K-mount Pentax cameras. These come in two varieties—"auto," which transfers the lens aperture information, and "manual," which requires that the photographer control the aperture manually.

Screw-Mount Extension Tubes

Manual Extension Tube Set: This is a set of three rings, 9.5mm, 19mm, and 28.5mm, which can be used individually or in any combination. When all three are used in conjunction with a 55mm Takumar lens, the film image is recorded at 1.17x.

Auto Extension Tube Set: This set is similar to the manual set, but it transfers the aperture information from the lens to the camera and permits automatic diaphragm operation.

Helicoid Extension Tube: This infinitely variable (from 16.8mm to 30.6mm) tube permits photography at magnifications from 0.30x to 0.7x when used with a 55mm lens.

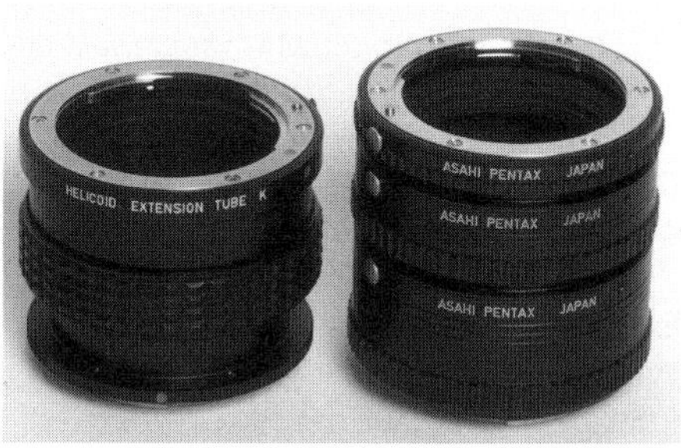

The Helicoid Extension Tube K (left) allows variable magnification. The Manual Extension Tube Set K (right) comes with three tubes that can be used individually or in combination to produce any level of magnification within the lens and tube combination's capability.

K-Mount Extension Tubes

Auto Extension Tube K 50mm: When used with the Pentax Macro 100mm f/4 lens, this extension tube yields magnifications from 0.5x to 1x (life size). It can be used with most K-mount lenses and allows the lens' automatic diaphragm and open-aperture meter system to function.

Auto Extension Tube K 100mm: This tube also permits both automatic diaphragm operation and open-aperture metering. It produces life-size images (or greater) when used with 100mm lenses, and 0.8x close-ups when used with lenses in the 120mm to 135mm range.

Auto Extension Tube Set K: This set of three extension tubes can be used individually or in any combination. Used with virtually any K-mount lens, they allow the convenience of automatic diaphragm operation plus open-aperture metering.

Manual Extension Tube Set K: This set provides the same range of image magnification as the Auto Extension Tube Set K, but the photographer must control the diaphragm manually and use stop-down metering techniques.

Helicoid Extension Tube K: This tube provides variable magnifications from 0.47x to 0.99x when used in conjunction with a 55mm lens.

Reverse Adapter

The Reverse Adapter screws into the lens' filter threads and allows the lens to be mounted in reverse (hence the name). This simple adapter provides greater than life-size images with a normal lens. There are actually three reverse adapters, the Reverse Adapter and two Reverse Adapter Ks. The Reverse Adapter allows lenses with 49mm filter threads to be mounted to a screw-mount camera. The Reverse Adapter K comes in two versions, one mounts lenses with 49mm filter threads to a K-mount body, and the other accepts lenses with 52mm diameter lens threads.

Bellows

Bellows systems offer great close-up flexibility. The bellows manufactured by Pentax are sturdy, well-made, and relatively easy to use. Pentax bellows are made to fit either K-mount or Pentax screw-mount cameras. While some allow for automatic diaphragm operation, others require that the aperture be controlled manually. There are other model differences, but those have to do with construction and style. What follows is a brief description of the various bellows offered by Pentax during this early SLR era.

Bellows Unit I: This single-rail bellows is used with screw-mount cameras and lenses. It offers magnifications of 0.62x to 2.45x when used in conjunction with a standard 55mm Takumar lens.

Bellows Unit II (Screw-mount version): This double-track bellows functions with screw-mount cameras and lenses, allowing for magnifications greater than 3x life size.

Bellows Unit II (K-mount version): This non-automatic K-mount bellows has an extension range from 32mm to 137mm. It employs a heavy-duty monorail like the Auto Bellows M and contains a movable tripod receptacle.

Slide Copier: This device attaches to the front of the Bellows Unit II (both screw-mount and K-mount versions) and conveniently allows you to make duplicate slides, slides from negatives, and negatives from slides.

Auto Bellows M and K: These monorail bellows function with K-mount cameras and lenses. When used with their Double Cable Releases, they provide automatic diaphragm operation. Their minimum extension is 38mm; full extension is 170mm, and they come with two magnification scales, one for a 50mm lens and another for a 55mm. The K bellows was produced for the K-series lenses and the M bellows for the M-series lenses. However, the only real difference between the Auto Bellows M and K is that the M version was supplied with a 49mm to 52mm step-up ring. The Double Cable Releases that came with the two bellows differ only in cosmetics.

The Auto Bellows M offers extension from 38mm to 170mm. A Double Cable Release stops down the aperture and releases the shutter.

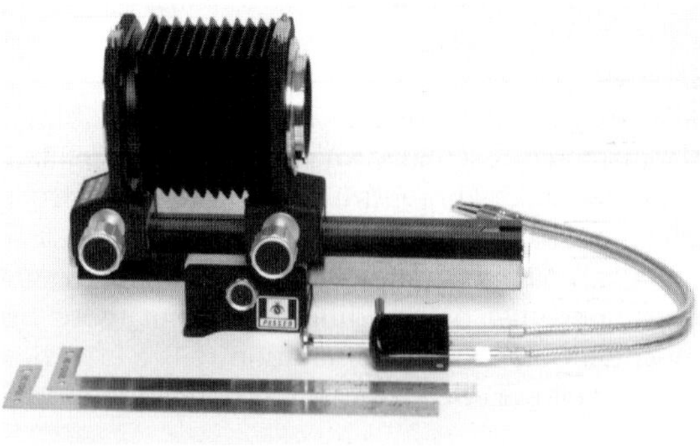

Slide Copier M and K: These slide copiers attach to the Auto Bellows M or K, respectively, for quick, accurate slide duplication.

Cable Releases Type 30 and 50

Aside from the Double Cable Release used with the Auto Bellows, Pentax also offers two conventional cable releases, the Type 30 Cable Release (30 cm long) and the Type 50 Cable Release (50 cm). Both have a locking feature so that the shutter can be locked open for long time exposures in "B."

Slide Holders

Pentax produced two rigid slide copying units that, when used with the proper extension tube(s) and/or bellows, make slide duplication easy.

Slide Holder 1x, K: This K-series slide holder allows the photographer to produce 1:1 (1x) slide duplicates.

Slide Holder K: This unit is more versatile than the Slide Holder 1x, K because it allows the photographer to make cropped duplicates in a broader range of magnifications, from 1.1x to 1.15x.

Copy Stands

A copy stand resembles an enlarger without an enlarging head. It consists of a baseboard, vertical column, and a mounting bracket that accepts any camera through its tripod socket.

Copipod: This copy stand has four telescoping legs and comes in a small black storage pouch. In use, the camera and lens are mounted to it with either a 46mm or 49mm lens filter thread adapter. Mounted on the Copipod, the camera sits horizontally over the object to be photographed, usually artwork, documents, or photographs.

Copy Stand, Deluxe Copy Stand II, Copy Stand III, and IIIP: The Pentax unit simply called "Copy Stand" allows you to mount the camera directly to its cross arm. The Deluxe Copy Stand II has a simplified macro focusing rail at the end of its cross arm. The Copy Stand III is a later version of the Copy Stand II, with essentially the same features. The Copy Stand IIIP (P, as in Portable) has a baseboard that folds to become the unit's carrying case.

The accessory Table Clamp secures a copy stand to a table, eliminating the need for a baseboard.

Macrophoto Stand and Lighting Table: This tiny, specialized copy stand is ideal for photographing small objects. It can be used with a camera equipped with a macro lens, extension tube(s), bellows, or any combination of close-up devices. Depending on the accessories that are used (e.g., Macro Focus Rail III or Auto Bellows M), it can yield magnifications ranging from 1/2x to 3.1x. It comes with a reversible stage plate that is 18% gray on one side and black on the other.

A "trans-illuminating" Lighting Stand is available, which replaces the stage plate so that work to be copied can be illuminated from below. It contains a built-in tungsten light source, but alternate light sources can also be employed. Optional 35mm and 6 x 7-format Slide Carriers make this an excellent system for slide and film duplication.

The Macrophoto Stand makes it easy to shoot tiny objects close-up. This one has the Macro Focus Rail III mounted to the stand. The stand is mounted to a Lighting Table and can be used for slide duplication because it allows light to be projected through an object from below. Other accessories include the Mechanical Stage and Slide Carrier, pictured here.

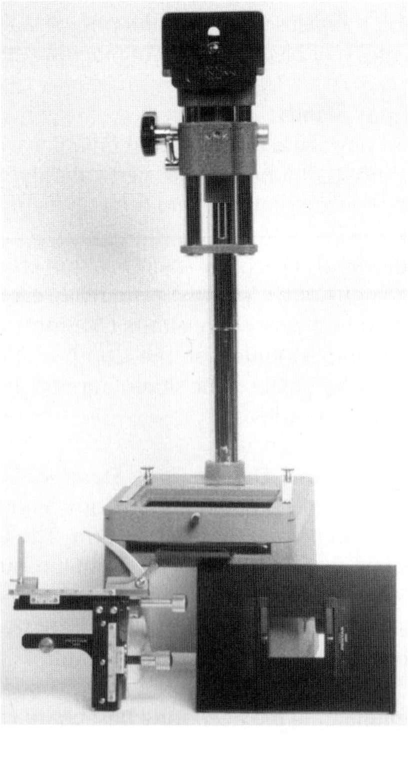

Macro Focus Rail III: This dual-track focusing rail fits between the camera and tripod. It has a fine focus adjuster that allows you to accurately move the entire camera system forward or backward without changing focus and/or magnification.

Microscope Adapter K/S

This adapter fits between a Pentax camera body and a microscope's optical tube. Photography through a microscope employs the microscope's optics, not conventional photographic lenses. This adapter connects a Pentax body to any microscope that uses a 25mm tube.

Microscope Lens Adapter K

The Microscope Lens Adapter K is used to adapt special-purpose lenses to the Pentax K mount. When special Olympus-manufactured lenses (i.e., Mplan and Zuiko Macro lenses) are used with this adapter and the appropriate Pentax close-up device (bellows and/or extension tubes), they can yield magnifications ranging from 2x to 10x.

Viewing Accessories

Eyecup II and Eyecup M

Eyecups help eliminate stray light from entering the viewfinder. They are primarily intended for use by people who don't wear eyeglasses, because glasses keep the viewfinder away from the eye and the additional distance caused by the eyecup may be detrimental. The Eyecup II is compatible with the Pentax Spotmatics, K2, K1000, KM, and KX cameras. The Eyecup M fits the Pentax ME, ME Super, MEF, MX, MG, MV, MV-1, and LX.

SMC Correction Lenses M

Pentax issued correction lenses in 8 diopters: –5, –4, –3, –2, –1, +1, +2, and +3. Use the ones designated "M" on the LX and M-series cameras and the ones without a designation on the Spotmatic, K2, K1000, KM, and KX cameras.

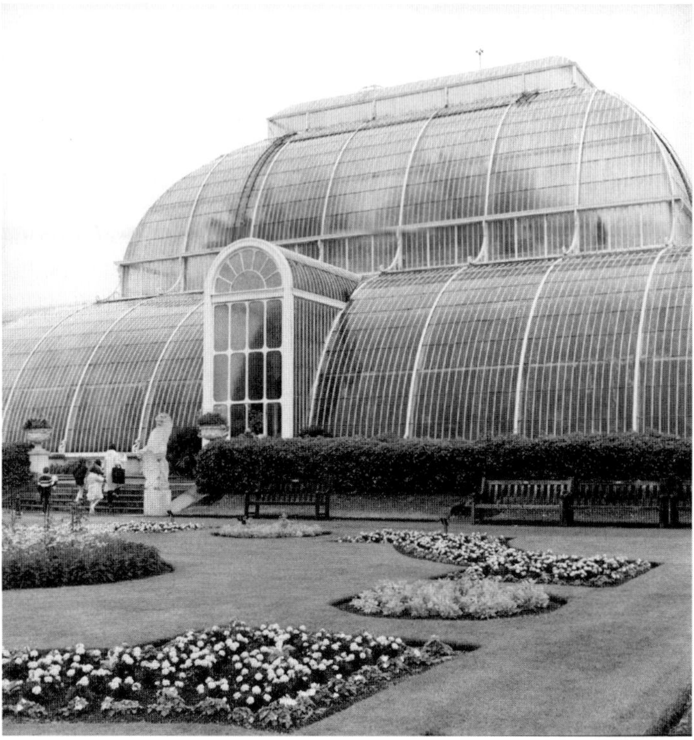

When shooting in bright sunlight, an eyecup can help reduce the light from entering the viewfinder.

Magnifier and Magnifier M

The Magnifier without an "M" designation slips into the grooves on the eyepiece, and magnifies the viewed image by a factor of 2. It is hinged and can be swung up out of the way so the entire focusing screen can be viewed without completely removing the magnifier. It has a chrome mount and is compatible with all Spotmatic cameras as well as the Pentax K2, K1000, KM, and KX. Other Pentax and other brand cameras can be used with this magnifier as well; if it fits, it will function correctly.

The Magnifier M is identical to the earlier Magnifier, however it has a black mount and is designed for use with the Pentax ME, ME Super, MEF, MX, MG, MV, MV-1, and LX.

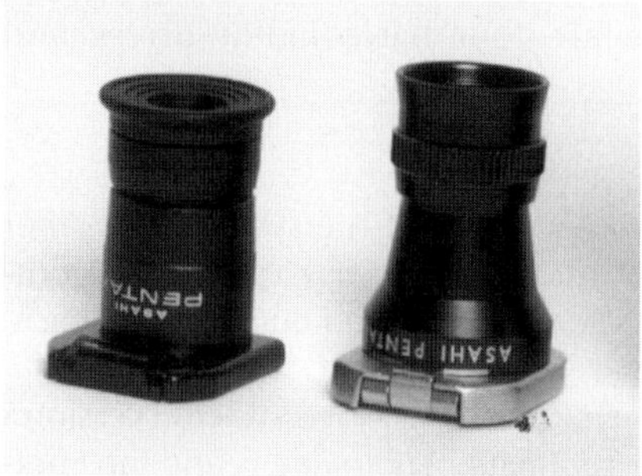

The Magnifier M (left) and Magnifier K (right) are two popular viewfinder accessories. The magnifiers enlarge the viewfinder image to aid in critical focusing. They can also be swung up for full viewfinder viewing.

Right-Angle Finders

In some literature, Pentax refers to right-angle finders as "refconverters," an abbreviation for "reflex converter." A right-angle finder does what its name implies and is a great tool for using with a camera mounted to a copy stand, microscope, or telescope.

Refconverter: This economy model finder does not yield a corrected image. The view is not inverted top to bottom, but is reversed left to right. If used with a camera that contains data (aperture readout or shutter speed) in the viewfinder, the data will appear reversed (mirror image). It was designed for use with the KM, K1000, and all Spotmatic cameras.

Refconverter M: This accessory contains a diopter adjustment and a rubber eyecup. It has a 2x magnifier that can be employed with the flip of a switch. Use this right-angle finder with the Pentax ME, ME Super, MEF, MG, MX, MV, MV-1, and LX cameras.

Refconverter II: This angle finder is like the Refconverter M, but lacks a 2x magnifier. Its image is corrected. It is intended for use with the Pentax K2 or KX. It will also function with the KM, K1000, and many screw-mount cameras.

Motor Drives and Motor Winders

Some of the cameras detailed in this book accept an optional accessory that advances the film automatically by using a battery-driven mechanism. There are four basic motor drives and four winders.

Asahi Pentax Motor Drive

This is much more than a motor drive—it is a system. The other motor drives that followed imitated this drive, offering a complete array of accessories to complement and augment the basic motor drive.

There are actually two versions of this drive system. Version I is designed for use with the Spotmatic, Spotmatic F, and the Spotmatic II. Version II functions with the Pentax KM, KX, and ES II. Each version fits these cameras and the 250-exposure back (a bulk-film magazine).

All of the above variations are capable of single-frame exposure and continuous speeds up to 3 frames per second (fps) at shutter speeds of 1/60 to 1/1000 second.

The power source options include 8 AA-size batteries, providing up to 1,500 exposures per set of carbon batteries (no data are available for alkalines); a 12v NiCd (nickel-cadmium) rechargeable battery system, providing up to 2,000 frames per charge; other 12v DC sources; or an AC power supply.

Some of the accessories for this system include the above-mentioned bulk-film magazine, different power sources, NiCd batteries, battery checker, battery chargers, bulk-film loaders, relay pack, hardwire remote control, wireless remote control, and an intervalometer.

Motor Drive MD

This motor drive fits the Pentax K2 DMD. It was manufactured only in a "Set 36" configuration (meaning that it takes only up to a 36-exposure roll); no 250-exposure back is available for this motor drive.

Capable of single-frame or continuous operation, the Motor Drive MD has a top speed of two frames per second (2 fps). A sliding scale allows the photographer to select a firing rate from one frame every two seconds up to two frames per second. The maximum speed can be achieved at shutter speeds as slow as 1/60 second.

Power to drive this unit is obtained from 12 AA batteries, a NiCd rechargeable system, alternate DC power supplies, or an AC power source.

Motor Drive MX

As its name implies, this motor is used exclusively with the Pentax MX. It is capable of single exposure operation and rapid sequence photography up to five frames per second (5 fps).

The motor can be set to expose one frame each time the trigger is depressed, or in its continuous mode, fire at any rate between 0.5 fps to 5 fps. This top speed can be achieved at any shutter speed of 1/60 second or faster.

The standard Battery Grip M operates on 12 AA batteries and is capable of driving up to 100 36-exposure rolls of film per set of alkaline power cells. The NiCd Battery Pack M will drive up to 40 36-exposure rolls per charge. The AC Power Pack M functions as long as power is supplied and contains a built-in timer for interval or time-lapse photography.

The accessory 250-exposure back and remote control release add to the versatility of the MX Motor Drive system.

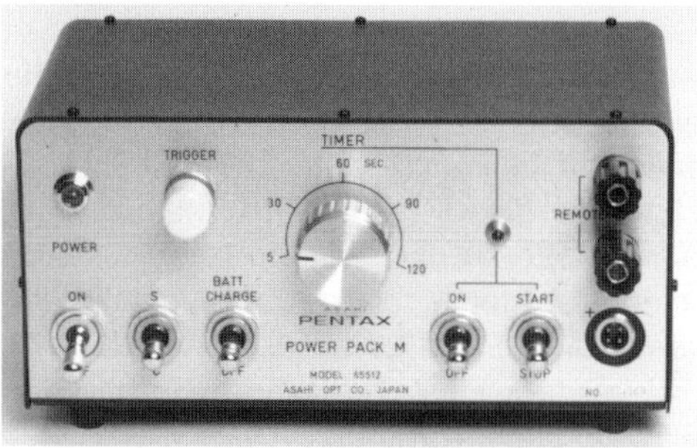

The Power Pack M is just one of the power sources that can be used to drive the MX or LX Motor Drives.

Motor Drive LX

This sophisticated motor drive contains a four-position dial for continuous film advance (C), single-frame advance (S), power rewind (R), and lock (L). An inner thumb wheel controls the firing rate (from 0.5 fps to 5 fps) when the motor is in the continuous (C) mode.

The Pentax Motor Drive LX can be powered with 12 AA batteries, an 18v Battery Grip M, 15v DC NiCd Battery Pack M, or the AC Power Pack M.

Fresh alkaline AA-size batteries will drive approximately 30 rolls of 36-exposure film, NiCds will function for about 20

The Motor Drive LX (front) can be powered by the Battery Grip M (back) or the NiCd Battery Pack (right).

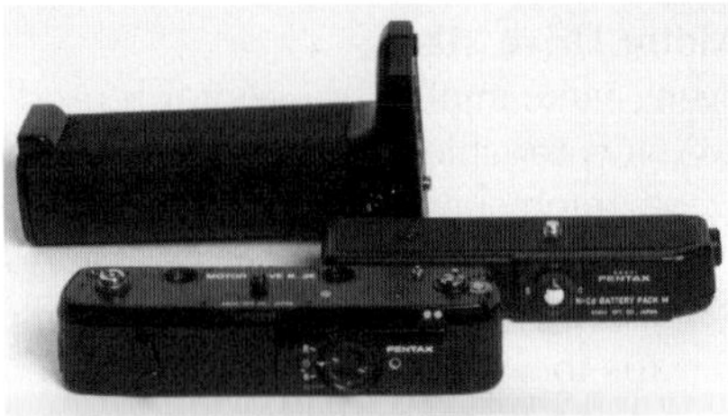

The small Coupler LX (center left) permits the Bulk-Film Magazine LX to be used with the LX without a motor drive. Two film cartridges are also pictured.

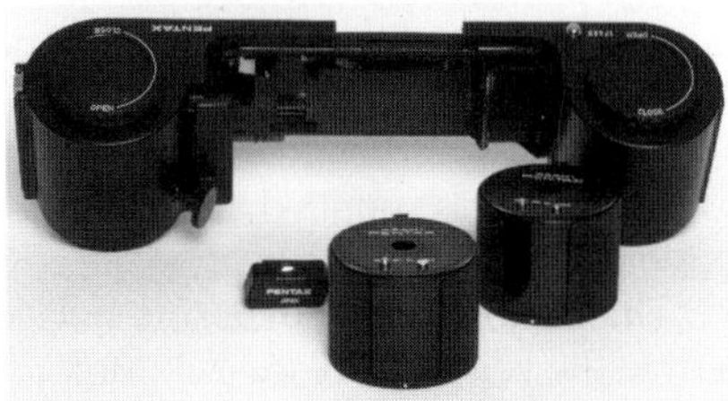

36-exposure rolls per charge, and an AC source will power the motor drive indefinitely.

The major components of the Pentax Motor Drive LX include a NiCd Battery Pack LX, Power Pack M, Motor Drive Remote Control Cord LX, Battery Grip M, Power Cord M (3 meters [9.8 feet]), Power Cord M (10 meters [32.8 feet]), Charge Pack M, Bulk-Film Magazine LX, Bulk-Film Cartridge, and Cartridge Loader 250.

Winder ME

The Winder ME was designed for use with the Pentax ME; its performance with other models may be less than perfect. It can function with the Pentax ME, ME Super, MG, and MV-1. (Individual camera-winder combinations should be tested.) It can be switched from single-frame (S) to continuous (C). In the "C" mode it will fire at a rate up to 1.5 fps (at shutter speeds of 1/60 second or faster).

The power source for the Winder ME is 6 AA-size batteries; manganese batteries will drive up to 20 36-exposure rolls, alkaline batteries as many as 150 36-exposure rolls, and lithium batteries should increase that number significantly.

Winder ME II

This winder will function with the Pentax ME, ME Super, MEF,

MG, and MV-1, plus newer cameras not covered in this book (Program, Program Plus, Super Program, etc.).

A switch on the winder grip allows for single-frame (S) or continuous (C) operation, with a maximum speed of 2 fps at shutter speeds of 1/60 second or faster.

Four AA-size batteries supply power; photographers can choose from manganese, alkaline, lithium, or NiCd batteries. A fresh set of manganese-oxide batteries will transport up to 20 36-exposure rolls.

Winder MX

This winder was designed for the Pentax MX camera. It is driven by four AA batteries. The number of rolls that can be shot per battery set is determined by several factors, the most important being the type of power cell employed. Lithium batteries deliver the most rolls per set, alkaline cells are a distant second, followed by carbon batteries; the NiCd cells drive the fewest number of rolls, but can be recharged.

The Winder MX has an S/C switch to select single-frame or continuous firing. The fastest firing rate of the Pentax Winder MX is 2 fps.

Winder LX

This winder is designed exclusively for the Pentax LX. Its three-position switch allows for continuous exposure operation up to 2 fps, single-frame operation, and a power "off" position.

The Winder LX functions at all speeds from 125 seconds to 1/2000 second in the camera's Automatic mode, and all speeds from 4 seconds to 1/2000 second in the camera's Manual mode.

Four AA batteries power this winder; because it performs an additional heavy-drain function, a new set of alkaline batteries will transport approximately 20 36-exposure rolls of film. ME, ME II, and MX winders drive about the same number of rolls when powered with manganese-oxide batteries as does this winder when loaded with alkaline power cells.

The Winder LX depletes power sooner because of its power film rewind feature. Though most motor drives automatically rewind film, virtually no other winder does. The power rewind lever activates the rewind function, causing a 36-exposure roll to be completely rewound in fewer than 10 seconds.

Data Backs

Data backs imprint information on film, usually in the lower portion of the frame. The exception is the LX Watch Data Back. Data typically imprinted by most data backs include the year, month, date, time of day, lens setting, shutter speed, or film speed.

Caution: *If you are contemplating purchasing a used data back, check the year function. Many data backs will not record more than a span of ten or twelve years. If a data back cannot print the current year or any of the years during which you intend to use your camera, there may be no replacement component that can modernize it.*

Dial Data Backs

The following three data backs are almost identical, except for the cameras they fit:

Dial Data ME: Functions properly with the Pentax ME, ME Super, MEF, and MG. Also functions with the MV and MV-1 when used in conjunction with the Hot Shoe Adapter 2P. Cameras not covered in this book that accept the Dial Data ME include the Super Program and Program Plus.

Dial Data MX: Functions with the Pentax MX

Dial Data LX: Functions with the Pentax LX

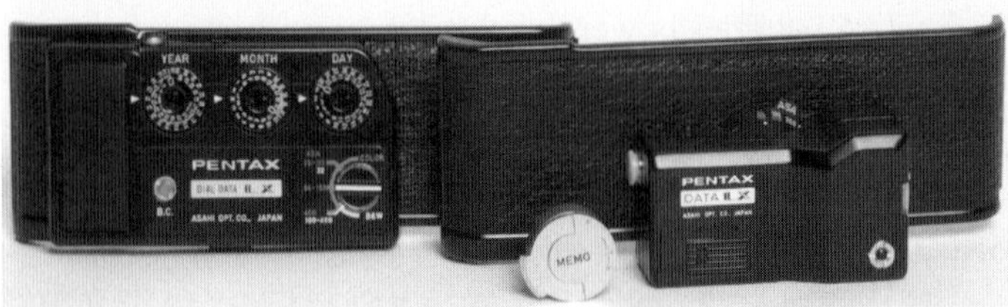

The Dial Data LX, designed for the Pentax LX, can be used to record information on the film frame such as exposure data or the date an image was taken. Dial data backs were also made for the Pentax ME and MX cameras.

These data backs have three clearly marked dials on their backs, one each for year, month, and day. Below the "day" dial is a film speed dial. This dial must be set because it controls the density of the printed data on the film. If the dial is set incorrectly, the data may be unreadable.

In the center of the data back is the easily identifiable nameplate. Next to the nameplate is the battery-check button, and next to that is the battery compartment cover.

All data backs require power; these backs derive power from three 1.5v alkaline or silver-oxide (S76) batteries located behind the battery door. How the power reaches the camera differs on all three of the backs.

The Dial Data ME and the Dial Data MX contain a connecting cord with a standard PC terminal. The Dial Data MX cord should be plugged into the FP terminal on the face of the camera. The Dial Data ME connecting cord must be plugged into the X terminal on the ME and ME Super. On cameras like the MV and MV-1, an accessory hot shoe adapter must be inserted into the camera's hot shoe, then the data back's cord is plugged into the adapter's PC outlet. Neither the Dial Data ME nor MX has an on/off switch. The ME and MX backs will not imprint data if their connecting cord is unplugged.

The Dial Data LX requires no connecting cord; it makes contact through two contact points that mate with corresponding terminals inside the LX camera's back. Unlike the other two Dial Datas, the Dial Data LX contains an on/off switch. If a back is installed but the user does not want data printed on a frame, the switch must be turned to "off."

Digital Data M

This versatile back fits the Pentax ME, ME Super, MV, MV-1, MG, and MEF with the supplied PC cord, plus the Super Program and Program Plus (not covered in this book). The Digital Data M has three imprinting modes: the first imprints year, month, and day (its calendar is programmed through the year 2019); the second imprints hour and minute; and the third offers no imprint (off).

This unit is powered by two S76 batteries, which will last for approximately 5,000 recordings or the duration of the batteries' shelf life (approximately one year). It contains a built-in battery check and an ISO dial to adjust data exposure. A six-digit liquid crystal display (LCD) allows the photographer to check status at a glance.

LX Watch Data

Manufactured exclusively for the Pentax LX, this back actually imprints a clock face in the upper left corner of the image. It will record the date, hour, minute, and second. The watch is interchangeable with a ground glass data-recording plate, on which any data can be penciled into a data-recording area.

A flashing LED on the back of the unit confirms imprint at the moment of exposure. One 6v silver-oxide, alkaline, or lithium battery (544, PX28, or equivalent) powers all the back's functions; a battery is good when the LED flashes as the battery check is depressed.

When the LX Watch Data back is in place and functioning, a built-in film blind in the camera must be moved into place to block the recording area. The imprinted data are registered in an otherwise unexposed area of the film.

Interchangeable Focusing Screens

Usually, a manufacturer will supply each SLR camera model with a focusing screen that performs best with that camera under most conditions. Under special situations, other focusing screens will make focusing, composing, and aligning the subject easier. At one time, Pentax offered factory-changeable screens for some camera models and user-changeable screens for others. If a person could locate a factory-changeable screen today, the cost would probably outweigh the desire.

The Pentax MX and the Pentax LX are designed to allow for user-changeable screens. Many of the screens made for the different camera models are similar in feature and function, but, for example, a screen for an MX should not be used in an LX, and vice versa. One exception is the SD-11, which fits both. If any other LX screen is used in an MX camera, the light meter will function incorrectly. If an MX screen is used in an LX camera the meter will function correctly, but the viewfinder image will be noticeably darker than that produced with an LX screen.

At one time, camera purchasers could special-order a Pentax Spotmatic IIa, Spotmatic II, SP 500, SL, or Motor Drive Spotmatic with a focusing screen other than the standard one supplied. The available screens included a matte ground glass screen, clear center spot with cross microprism, split-image rangefinder (with no microprism), and a special microprism screen that functions with slower lenses, when focusing is less critical.

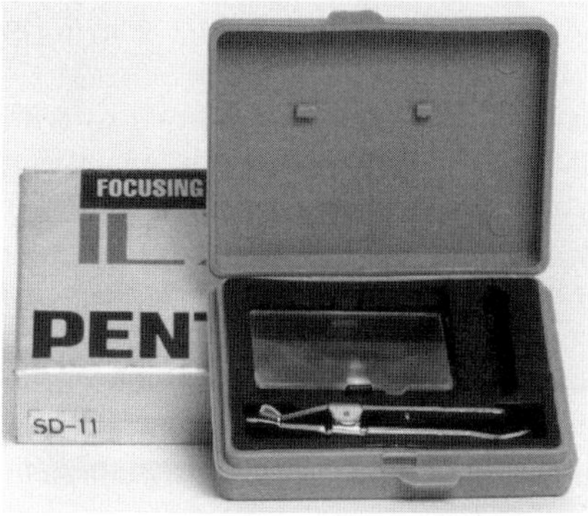

An SD-11 Focusing Screen was designed for the Pentax MX and LX cameras. It came with a set of tweezers to make screen replacement easy.

MX Focusing Screens

SA-1: A matte screen with microprism center. Ideal for moderately fast lenses.

SA-3: Same as the SA-1, but intended for use with lenses that have maximum apertures of f/2.8 or faster.

SB-1: Split-image rangefinder centered on a matte screen. Intended for general use.

SC-1: The standard screen supplied as original equipment when the camera came from the factory. It contains a central split-image spot with a microprism doughnut on a matte field.

SD-1: Matte screen with cross hairs. Ideal for use with high-magnification photography.

SD-11: Clear glass focusing screen with central cross hairs. Ideal for low-light photography and high-magnification photography.

SE: Matte screen only. Works well with slow lenses, dense filters, and low-light situations.

SG: Matte screen with vertical and horizontal lines. Used for object alignment, as in architectural photography.

SI: Matte screen with engraved scales. Facilitates the calculation of image size.

Pentax LX Focusing Screens

SA-21: Microprism center on a matte field. Intended for use in general and low-light situations.

SA-23: Similar to the SA-21, but for use with f/1.2 to f/2.8 lenses.

SA-26: Microprism on a matte field. Designed for use with 300mm lenses or longer. Works well with lenses that have a maximum aperture of f/8 or faster.

SA-32: Contains a microprism field with no other surface feature. Designed for high-magnification photography, such as extreme close-up or long telephoto shots.

SA-37: Contains the same features as the SA-32, but for use with 200mm to 1200mm lenses.

SB-21: Split-image focusing spot on a matte field. Ideal for general photography.

SC-21: Standard factory-installed screen containing a central split-image rangefinder, microprism collar, and matte screen field.

SC-26: Split-image focusing spot surrounded by a microprism doughnut on a matte field. Looks identical to the SC-21, but designed for use with lenses 300mm or longer.

SD-11: Identical to the SD-21, but with a clear glass field.

SD-21: All-matte focusing screen with central cross hairs. Ideal for low-light photography and high-magnification photography.

SE-20: All-matte screen. Designed for use with small-aperture telephoto lenses.

SE-25: Similar to the SE-20, but formulated for use with lenses 300mm or longer.

SG-20: Matte screen with vertical and horizontal lines spaced at 6mm intervals. Often called the architecture screen, it is also ideal for copying documents and artwork.

SI-20: Matte screen with vertical and horizontal scales. Ideal for determining image size.

Pentax LX Interchangeable Viewfinders and Eyepieces

The Pentax LX is designed so that its viewfinder can be removed and replaced with several other finders. Only high-end professional cameras offer this luxury. Once a photographer has used a camera with several finders, it is difficult to be happy with a camera that does not have interchangeable prisms.

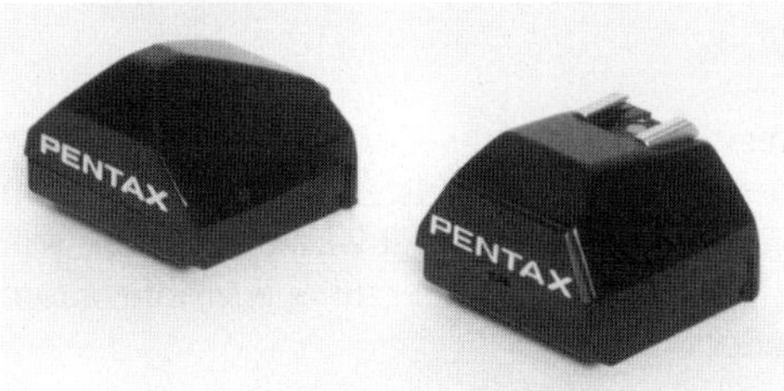

FA-2 (left) and FA-1 (right) Eye-Level Finders

FA-1 Eye-Level Pentaprism Finder

This viewfinder is probably the most commonly used LX viewfinder. It features a built-in diopter correction feature, full-information viewfinder display, and built-in hot shoe.

FA-1W Eye-Level Pentaprism Finder

This finder is identical to the FA-1, with two exceptions: The FA-1 yields a 0.9x image, while the FA-1W produces a 0.84x image and has an extended range of diopter correction. The FA-1 corrects the diopter through the range of –1.5 to 0; the FA-1W corrects from –3 to +1. A greater diopter correction range is available by using separate eyepiece correction lenses.

FA-2 Eye-Level Finder

This finder is identical to the FA-1 finder, with two exceptions: It does not have a hot shoe, and it lacks an aperture readout window.

FE-1 Waist-Level Finder

This waist-level finder contains a high-magnification focusing eyepiece. Its diopter is adjustable through the range of –5 to +4. All viewfinder data, except the f/stop setting, are visible but reversed. It is ideal for use when critical focus is important.

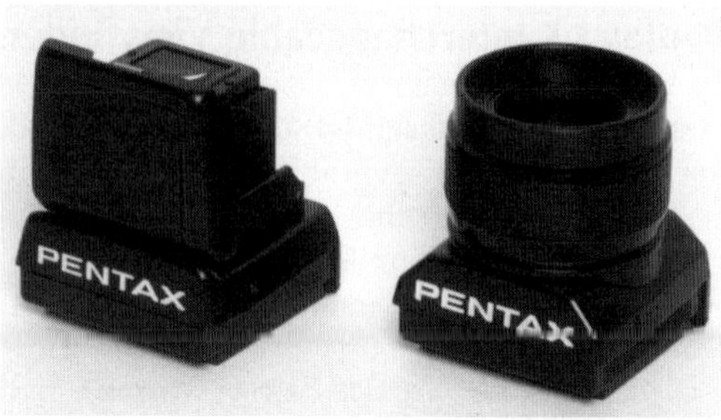

FF-1 (left) and FE-1 (right) Waist-Level Finders

FF-1 Waist-Level Finder

This conventional waist-level finder folds very flat when not in use and pops up to exclude much stray light when it is in use. All viewfinder information except the aperture setting is visible, albeit reversed, when this finder is used.

FB-1 Finder System Base

This unique system accepts any of three optional eyepieces that bayonet onto the rear of the prism housing. This system, in any configuration, offers full-information viewing.

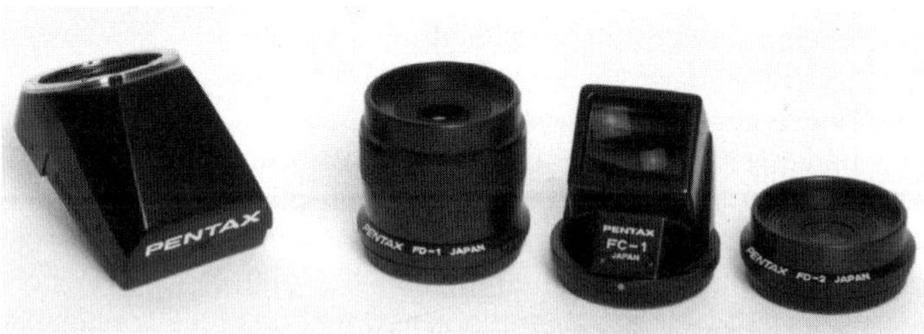

FB-1 Finder, FD-1 Magni Eyepiece, FC-1 Action Eyepiece, and FD-2 Standard Eyepiece

FC-1 Action Eyepiece

This eyepiece has extremely long eye relief, making it an excellent tool for sports and action photography. It also rotates 180°, so it is an excellent system for use on copy stands, microscopes, or telescopes.

FD-1 Magni Eyepiece

This magnifying eyepiece converts the FB-1 to a 45° viewing system. It contains a diopter correction range from –4.5 to +3.5.

FD-2 Standard Eyepiece
This eyepiece provides a standard 45° viewing angle. It does not magnify or contain any diopter correction.

Pentax LX Grips

Pentax designed two grips for the LX, the Accessory Grip A and the Accessory Grip B. They are designed to be attached to the lugs located on the camera face just below the film advance lever, and they screw into the socket provided. Accessory Grip A is a block that can be whittled by the camera user to any custom contour. Accessory Grip B is a factory-contoured hand grip.

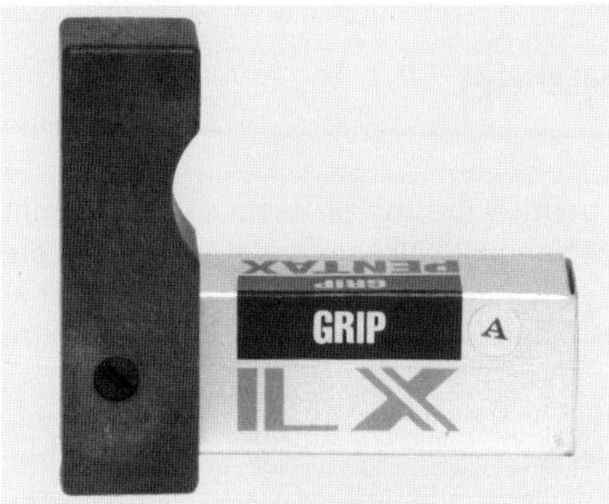

Pentax makes two grips for the LX. Accessory Grip A (shown) can be custom-shaped to perfectly match the photographer's own hand grip, Grip B is shaped by the factory.

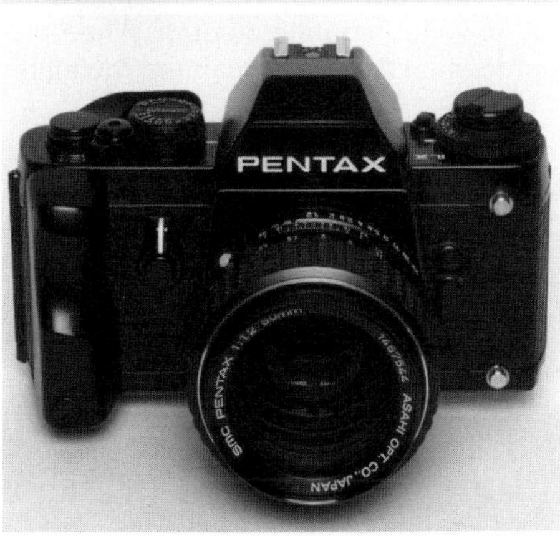

Here, the LX is shown with an accessory Grip B attached.

Camera Cases

With every camera model, Pentax offered several cases: "ever-ready" cases, cases with long snouts, cases for cameras with a winder, cases for cameras with a data back, gadget bags, and even metal-covered cases.

Most photographers do not use the case that was made for their camera (although some collectors do). Some cameras listed in this book have outlived their carrying cases, and most cases manufactured for these cameras have long been discontinued. If you need a case for camera protection, look in the used and aftermarket sections of your local camera store. Try any case that is the right size; cases from other camera manufacturers are frequently compatible.

Miscellaneous Accessories

Mount Adapter K

The Mount Adapter K permits the use of Pentax screw-mount lenses on cameras with a K-mount. When screw-mount lenses are used with this adapter, they become fully manual lenses. That means that no automatic diaphragm control or open-aperture metering is possible.

6 x 7 Lens Mount Adapter K

The 6 x 7 Lens Mount Adapter K allows Pentax 6 x 7 lenses to be used on 35mm K-mount (bayonet-mount) cameras. When this adapter is used, the diaphragm action is manual and the meter

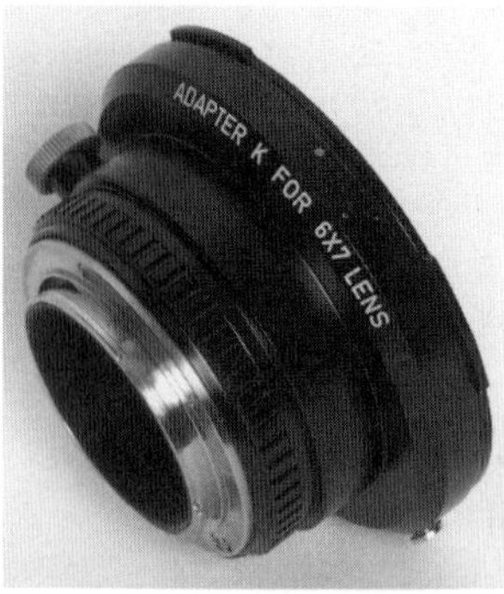

6 x 7 Lens Mount Adapter K

reading must be taken in the stopped-down mode. When it is used with a long telephoto lens, the camera can be turned vertically or horizontally while the lens remains mounted on the tripod.

Rear Converter K T6–2X

This device is simply a K-mount 2x teleconverter designed to be used with lenses in the 135mm to 300mm focal-length range. It retains the automatic diaphragm action and the open-aperture metering functions of automatic diaphragm lenses. It almost doubles the lens' focal length, while diminishing the lens' speed by 2 stops.

49mm and 52mm Stereo Adapter

These two adapters are designed for use with 50mm and 55mm lenses. They produce two images on a single frame and provide the proper offset viewpoint that produces three-dimensional images when viewed with the proper stereo viewer.

Stereo Adapter Set

The original Stereo Adapter was sold in a set, consisting of a stereo-lens system and Stereo Viewer I (it was not actually designated "I"). This stereo set was issued when the Spotmatic was in production.

Stereo Viewer II

This stereo viewer was designed to view slides made with the Pentax Stereo Lens Adapters described above.

90 Degree Mirror Adapter

During the early Pentax SLR era, Pentax offered a 90 Degree Mirror Adapter and a 90 Degree Mirror Adapter II. These mirror adapters screw on the front of the camera's taking lens and, through use of a mirror, photograph objects at 90° from the lens' axis. The difference in the two models consists mainly in their filter thread sizes. Today, step-up and step-down rings can couple most male and female thread sizes. These mirrors were designed for candid photography and generated much interest when they were introduced.

Pentax ME Belt Clip

This attachment offers the photographer an innovative way to carry a camera, by clipping it to a belt. It can be used with every

M-series camera in this book except the MX. The belt clip screws into the camera's tripod socket and fits the contour of the camera body. The wide clip presses against the camera's back. When not in use, it merely adds a little bulk to the camera, and does not get in the way of the camera's functions.

Finding Pentax Accessories

Over the years, Asahi continued to manufacture many other accessories that function with these Pentax classic cameras. If you are seeking an accessory such as the Infrared Remote Control System, any aftermarket device, or any of these classic accessories, check with your local camera store. Many have a used-equipment section, and you may be pleasantly surprised to find the piece you are looking for.